P9-CMS-894

The North American Third Edition

Cambridge Latin Course
Unit 1

Revision Editor
Ed Phinney
Chair, Department of Classics, & Director, University Foreign Language Resource Center
University of Massachusetts at Amherst, U.S.A.

Consulting Editor
Patricia E. Bell
Teacher of Latin & Assistant Head of Languages
Centennial Collegiate and Vocational Institute, Guelph, Ontario, Canada

Editorial Assistant
Barbara Romaine
Amherst, Massachusetts, U.S.A.

CAMBRIDGE
UNIVERSITY PRESS

Published by the Press Syndicate of the University of Cambridge
40 West 20th Street, New York, NY 10011-4211, USA

The Cambridge Latin Course was funded and developed by the
University of Cambridge School Classics Project and SCDC Publications,
London, and is published with the sponsorship of the School Curriculum
Development Committee in London and the North American Cambridge
Classics Project.

This edition first published 1988
Reprinted with corrections 1989
Reprinted 1990 (twice), 1992, 1993, 1994, 1995, 1996, 1997, 1998, 2000, 2003

Printed in the United States of America

Library of Congress cataloging in publication data
Cambridge Latin Course. Unit 1.
Includes index.
1. Latin language – Grammar – 1976-   . I Title:
Cambridge Latin course. Unit 1.   II. Title: Cambridge
Latin course. Unit one.
PA2087.5C3   1987   478.2'421   87-10281

ISBN 0-521-34379-8 hardback

Stories from Unit I which have been recorded on the cassette tapes accompanying
the course are so indicated by the cassette symbol ⟨oo⟩ .

Drawings by Joy Mellor, Leslie Jones, Peter Kesteven and Neil Sutton

Acknowledgements

Thanks are due to the following for permission to reproduce photographs: Ronald
Sheridan's Photo Library, front cover and pp 13, 93; Ed Phinney, pp iv, 53 top, 56, 64,
108; Metropolitan Museum of Art, New York, Rogers Fund, 1903, pp 9 (detail), 12,
17 (detail); Scala, pp 16, 61 top; Cambridge School Classics Project, pp 24, 25, 29, 34,
41, 44, 45, 61 bottom, 65, 73, 81, 84, 89, 97, 105, 112, 120, 124, 137, 141, 144; The
Mansell Collection, pp 28, 53 bottom, 79, 95, 199; The Royal Ontario Museum,
Toronto, p 60; The Trustees of the British Museum, p 80; Museo Teatrale alla Scala,
Milan, p 128; Werner Forman Archive, pp 132, 168; Edwin Smith, p 139; The J. Allan
Cash Photo Library, p 149; Ampliaciones y reproducciones MAS, p 156; The J. Paul
Getty Museum, Julius Shulman, p 165; The Photo Source, London, p 180; Yale Center
for British Art, Paul Mellon Collection, New Haven, Ct, p 193; National Geographic
Society, Washington, DC, p 196; The Imperial War Museum, London, p 198.

**The cover picture shows a detail from the Roman wall-paintings in the Villa of
the Mysteries in Pompeii.**

Contents

Front door of the House of Caecilius

Stage 1

2

Caecilius

Caecilius est pater.

Metella est māter.

Quīntus est fīlius.

Clēmēns est servus.

Grumiō est coquus.

Cerberus est canis.

Caecilius est in tablīnō.

Metella est in ātriō.

Quīntus est in triclīniō.

Clēmēns est in hortō.

Grumiō est in culīnā.

Cerberus est in viā.

pater est in tablīnō.
pater in tablīnō scrībit.

māter est in ātriō.
māter in ātriō sedet.

fīlius est in triclīniō.
fīlius in triclīniō bibit.

servus est in hortō.
servus in hortō labōrat.

coquus est in culīnā.
coquus in culīnā labōrat.

canis est in viā.
canis in viā dormit.

est	*is*	in triclīniō	*in the dining-room*
pater	*father*	in hortō	*in the garden*
māter	*mother*	in culīnā	*in the kitchen*
fīlius	*son*	in viā	*in the street*
servus	*slave*	scrībit	*is writing*
coquus	*cook*	sedet	*is sitting*
canis	*dog*	bibit	*is drinking*
in tablīnō	*in the study*	labōrat	*is working*
in ātriō	*in the reception hall*	dormit	*is sleeping*

Cerberus

Caecilius est in hortō. Caecilius in hortō sedet. servus est in ātriō. servus in ātriō labōrat. Metella est in ātriō. Metella in ātriō sedet. Quīntus est in tablīnō. Quīntus in tablīnō scrībit. Cerberus est in viā.

coquus est in culīnā. coquus in culīnā dormit. Cerberus intrat. 5
Cerberus circumspectat. cibus est in mēnsā. canis salit. canis in mēnsā stat. Grumiō stertit. canis lātrat. Grumiō surgit. coquus est īrātus. "pestis! furcifer!" coquus clāmat. Cerberus exit.

Words and Phrases

intrat	*enters*
circumspectat	*looks around*
cibus	*food*
in mēnsā	*on the table*
salit	*jumps*
stat	*stands*
stertit	*snores*
lātrat	*barks*
surgit	*gets up*
īrātus	*angry*
pestis!	*pest!*
furcifer!	*scoundrel!*
clāmat	*shouts*
exit	*goes out*

About the Language

1 Latin sentences containing the word **est** often follow an order similar to that of English.

for example:

Metella est māter.   canis est in viā.
Metella is the mother.   *The dog is in the street.*

2 In other Latin sentences, the order is usually different from that of English.

for example: canis in viā dormit.
                The dog is sleeping in the street.

                servus in culīnā labōrat.
                The slave is working in the kitchen.

Practicing the Language

1 Complete each sentence with a suitable word from the list below. Write out the completed sentence in Latin, and then translate it into English.

Quīntus, Grumiō, Caecilius, canis, māter, servus

for example: . . . . . . est in hortō.
                servus est in hortō.
                The slave is in the garden.

1 . . . . . . est in hortō.   4 . . . . . . est in tablīnō.
2 . . . . . . est in viā.   5 . . . . . . est in ātriō.
3 . . . . . . est in culīnā.   6 . . . . . . est in triclīniō.

2 Complete each sentence with a suitable phrase from the list below. Write out the completed sentence in Latin, and then translate it into English.

in viā, in hortō, in ātriō, in tablīnō, in culīnā, in triclīniō

1 Clēmēns . . . . . . labōrat.   4 Metella . . . . . . stat.
2 Caecilius . . . . . . scrībit.   5 coquus est . . . .
3 canis . . . . . . lātrat.   6 Quīntus est . . . .

Wall-painting from a villa near Pompeii

Caecilius

Caecilius lived in Italy during the first century A.D. in the town of Pompeii. This town had a population of about 20,000, and was situated at the foot of Mount Vesuvius on the coast of the Bay of Naples. Caecilius was a rich Pompeian banker. His business accounts, which were discovered when his house was dug up, tell us that he was also an auctioneer, tax-collector, farmer, and moneylender.

He inherited some of his money from his father, Lucius Caecilius Felix, but he probably obtained most of it through his own shrewd and energetic business activities. He dealt in slaves, cloth, timber, and property. He also carried on a cleaning and dyeing business, grazed herds of sheep or cattle on pastureland outside the town, and he

sometimes won the contract for collecting the local taxes. He may have owned a few stores as well, and probably lent money to local shipping companies wishing to trade with countries overseas. The profit on such trade was often very large.

We can discover more about Caecilius by studying his full name, which was Lucius Caecilius Iucundus. Only a Roman citizen would have three names. A slave would have only one, such as Clemens or Grumio. As a Roman citizen, Caecilius not only had the right to vote in elections, but also was fully protected by the law against unjust treatment. The slaves who lived and worked in his house and in his businesses had no rights of their own. They were his property, and he could treat them as well or as badly as he wished. There was one important exception to this rule. The law did not allow a master to put a slave to death without showing good reason.

Caecilius' first name was Lucius. This was the personal name of Caecilius himself, rather like a modern first name. His second name was Caecilius and this shows that he was a member of the "clan" of the Caecilii. Clans or family groups were very important, and strong feelings of loyalty existed within them. Caecilius' third name, Iucundus, is the name of his own family and close relatives. The word **iūcundus** means *pleasant*, just as in English we find surnames like Merry or Jolly. Whether Caecilius was in fact a pleasant character, you will find out from the stories that you read about him.

Metella

Caecilius' wife Metella, like many Roman wives and mothers, had an important position in her home. She was responsible for the management of the household, and had to supervise the work of the domestic slaves. Much skill in organization and a good deal of shrewdness were necessary if she was to keep everything running smoothly at home. She would also prepare carefully for social occasions and help to entertain guests.

Although the lives of married women were mainly centered on their houses, they would go out and about in the town, to visit friends, to shop, and to attend public events. Occasionally they managed their own businesses (see picture on page 61), although this was not common. A Pompeian woman named Eumachia, who donated the cost of the meeting hall of the cloth merchants on the southeast side of the forum (shown on page 53), successfully took over her father's pottery business after his death.

Metella is shown on page 5 with a distaff and spindle for spinning wool. In the centuries before Metella's lifetime most women would have learned to spin and to weave cloth for the clothes worn by their families. This skill was highly regarded and was sometimes mentioned on tombstones as one of a woman's virtues, as these lines from an inscription show.

> She loved her husband in her heart.
> She bore two sons; of these she leaves one on earth, the other she
>   placed beneath the earth.
> She looked after the house, she spun wool.

According to the historian Suetonius, the Emperor Augustus considered spinning and weaving activities worthy of women at the highest level of

Lady playing a cithara, from a wall-painting

Summer triclinium from a house in Herculaneum

society (although this was probably already an old-fashioned notion by his time):

> In bringing up his daughter and granddaughters, Augustus even made them get used to spinning . . . Except on special occasions, the Divine Augustus always wore ordinary clothes made by his sister, wife, daughter, or granddaughters.

Metella certainly did not need to make clothing for herself and her family, as she could purchase it ready-made from merchants in Pompeii (as she does in Stage 9). Nevertheless, she would very likely have learned as a girl the arts of spinning and weaving, and might have pursued them as a traditional pastime, much as people today enjoy knitting or sewing.

Houses in Pompeii

The house in which a wealthy man like Caecilius lived differed in several ways from a modern house. The house came right up to the sidewalk; there was no garden or grass in front of it. The windows were few, small, and placed fairly high up. They were intended to let in enough light, but to keep out the heat of the sun. Large windows would have made the rooms uncomfortably hot in summer and cold in winter.

The houses usually stood only one story high. Some houses in Pompeii, however, had a second story above. From the outside, with its few windows and high walls stretching all the way around, the house did not look very attractive or inviting. It was deliberately designed to shut out noise and heat, and to provide as much privacy as possible.

The ground plan of the house shows two parts or areas of about equal size. They look like courtyards surrounded by rooms opening off the central space. Let us look at these two parts more closely.

The main entrance to the house was in the side facing the street. It consisted of a tall double door. The Latin word for this door was **iānua**.

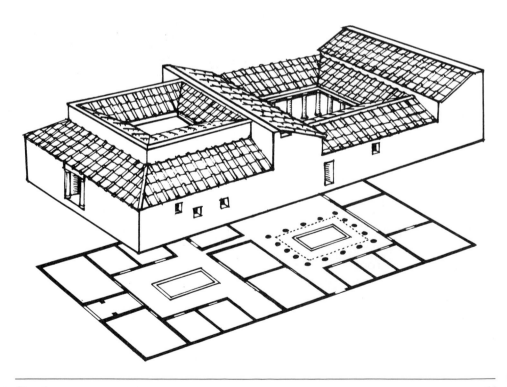

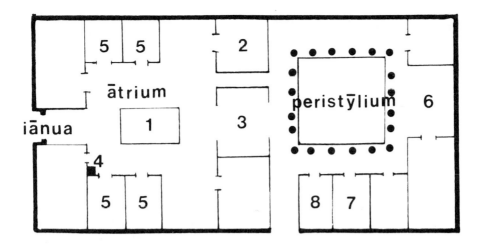

Plan of a Pompeian house

1	impluvium	pool for rainwater
2	triclīnium	dining-room
3	tablīnum	study
4	larārium	shrine of the household gods
5	cubiculum	bedroom
6	summer triclīnium	
7	culīna	kitchen
8	latrīna	toilet

On passing through the door, the visitor came into a short corridor, which led straight into the reception hall or **ātrium**. This was the most important part of the house. It was large and high and contained little furniture. The roof sloped down slightly towards a large square opening in the middle, called a **compluvium**. The light streamed in through the compluvium, high overhead. Immediately below was a shallow rectangular pool, called an **impluvium**, and lined with marble, which received the rainwater. Around the atrium were arranged the main rooms used by the master's family, the bedrooms, study, and dining-room. The entrances to these rooms were not usually provided with a wooden door, but with a heavy curtain that could be pulled across.

One of the most striking things about the atrium was the sense of space. The high roof with the glimpse of sky through the compluvium, the large floor area, and the sparse furnishings all helped to give this impression. The only furniture to be seen was a bronze or marble table, a couch, and a chest in which the family treasures were stored. In a corner, near the main door, there was a small shrine at which the family gods were worshiped. The floor was paved with plain marble slabs.

Three-legged table in the tablinum of the House of Paquius Proculus

The walls of the atrium were decorated with panels of brightly painted plaster. The Pompeians were especially fond of red, orange, and blue. On many of these panels there were paintings of scenes from well-known stories, especially the myths of the Greeks.

From this first area of the house, the visitor passed by way of the **tablīnum** (study) or through a passage into the second part. This was the **peristȳlium**. It was a garden surrounded by a colonnade of pillars. Around the colonnade were the kitchen, the toilet, the summer dining-room, slaves' quarters, and storage rooms. Some houses also had their own set of baths. Like the atrium, the colonnade was often elaborately decorated. In the center of this area was an ornamental garden, where flowers and shrubs were laid out in a careful plan. In the small fishpond in the middle, a fountain threw up a jet of water, and marble statues of gods and heroes stood here and there. In the peristylium, the members of the family enjoyed sunshine or shade as they wished; here they relaxed on their own or entertained a few close friends.

Only wealthy families could afford houses like this; most people lived in much simpler homes. Some of the poorer storekeepers had only a few rooms above their stores. In large cities such as Rome, many people lived in apartment buildings several stories high.

Couch in a cubiculum

Words and Phrases Checklist

You have now met the following words three times or more. Check that you are able to translate them.

ātrium	*atrium, reception hall*
canis	*dog*
coquus	*cook*
est	*is*
fīlius	*son*
hortus	*garden*
in	*in, on*
labōrat	*works, is working*
māter	*mother*
pater	*father*
sedet	*sits, is sitting*
servus	*slave*
via	*street*

Word Search

Match each definition with one of the words given below.

affiliate, canine, horticulturalist, laboratory, maternity, sedentary, service

1 . . . . . : a room or building used for scientific testing or research
2 . . . . . : a person who works with plants
3 . . . . . : motherhood
4 . . . . . : the act of providing goods or assistance
5 . . . . . : pertaining to dogs
6 . . . . . : tending to be inactive
7 . . . . . : to associate or join oneself

in vīllā

amīcus

Caecilius est in ātriō.

amīcus Caecilium salūtat.

Metella est in ātriō.

amīcus Metellam salūtat.

Quīntus est in ātriō.

amīcus Quīntum salūtat.

servus est in ātriō.

amīcus servum salūtat.

canis est in ātriō.

amīcus canem salūtat.

Metella

coquus est in culīnā.

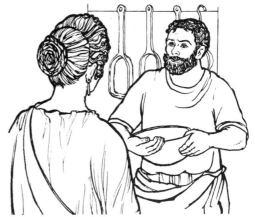

Metella culīnam intrat.

Grumiō labōrat.

Metella Grumiōnem spectat.

cibus est parātus.

Metella cibum gustat.

Grumiō est anxius.

Metella Grumiōnem laudat.

amīcus est in hortō.

Metella amīcum vocat.

mercātor

amīcus Caecilium vīsitat. amīcus est mercātor. mercātor vīllam
intrat. Clēmēns est in ātriō. Clēmēns mercātōrem salūtat. Caecilius
est in tablīnō. Caecilius pecūniam numerat. Caecilius est
argentārius. amīcus tablīnum intrat. Caecilius surgit.

"salvē!" Caecilius mercātōrem salūtat.   5

"salvē!" mercātor respondet.

Caecilius triclīnium intrat. amīcus quoque intrat. amīcus in lectō
recumbit. argentārius in lectō recumbit.

Grumiō in culīnā cantat. Grumiō pāvōnem coquit. coquus est
laetus. Caecilius coquum audit. Caecilius nōn est laetus. Caecilius 10
cēnam exspectat. amīcus cēnam exspectat. Caecilius Grumiōnem
vituperat.

Words and Phrases

mercātor	*merchant*
amīcus	*friend*
vīsitat	*is visiting*
vīllam	*house*
salūtat	*greets*
pecūniam ⎫ numerat ⎭	⎧ *is counting* ⎩ *money*
argentārius	*banker*
salvē!	*hello!*
respondet	*replies*
quoque	*also, too*
in lectō ⎫ recumbit ⎭	⎧ *reclines* ⎩ *on a couch*
cantat	*is singing*
pāvōnem	*peacock*
coquit	*is cooking*
laetus	*happy*
audit	*hears, listens to*
nōn est	*is not*
cēnam	*dinner*
exspectat	*is waiting for*
vituperat	*tells off, curses*

in triclīniō

Grumiō triclīnium intrat. Grumiō pāvōnem portat. Clēmēns triclīnium intrat. Clēmēns vīnum portat. Caecilius pāvōnem gustat.

"pāvō est optimus!" Caecilius clāmat.

mercātor quoque pāvōnem gustat. mercātor cēnam laudat. dominus coquum laudat. Grumiō exit.   5

ancilla intrat. ancilla suāviter cantat. ancilla dominum dēlectat. ancilla mercātōrem dēlectat. mox dominus dormit. amīcus quoque dormit.

Grumiō triclīnium intrat et circumspectat. coquus cibum in mēnsā videt. Grumiō cibum cōnsūmit et vīnum bibit! Caecilius   10
Grumiōnem nōn videt. coquus in triclīniō magnificē cēnat.

coquus ancillam spectat. ancilla Grumiōnem dēlectat. Grumiō ancillam dēlectat. Grumiō est laetissimus.

Words and Phrases

portat	*is carrying*	mox	*soon*
vīnum	*wine*	et	*and*
gustat	*tastes*	videt	*sees*
optimus	*very good, excellent*	cibum cōnsūmit	*eats the food*
laudat	*praises*	magnificē	*magnificently, in style*
dominus	*master*	cēnat	*eats dinner, dines*
ancilla	*slave-girl*	spectat	*looks at*
suāviter	*sweetly*	laetissimus	*very happy*
dēlectat	*pleases*		

About the Language

1 You have now met two forms of the same word:

Caecilius – Caecilium   Metella – Metellam
mercātor – mercātōrem

2 The different forms are known as the *nominative case* and the *accusative case*.

NOMINATIVE	ACCUSATIVE
Caecilius	Caecilium
Metella	Metellam
mercātor	mercātōrem

3 If Caecilius performs an action, such as praising Grumio, the nominative **Caecilius** is used:

Caecilius Grumiōnem laudat.
Caecilius praises Grumio.

4 But if somebody else does something to Caecilius, the accusative **Caecilium** is used:

amīcus Caecilium salūtat.
The friend greets Caecilius.

5 Notice the difference in word order between Latin and English:

coquus culīnam intrat.
The cook enters the kitchen.

Clēmēns vīnum portat.
Clemens carries the wine.

Practicing the Language

1 Complete each sentence with a suitable word or phrase from the list below. Write out the completed sentence in Latin, and then translate it into English.

scrībit, in culīnā, servus, amīcus, sedet, in viā

for example: canis . . . . . . stat.
     canis in viā stat.
     The dog is standing in the street.

1 Grumiō . . . . . . coquit.
2 . . . . . in hortō labōrat.
3 mercātor in tablīnō . . . . . .
4 Cerberus . . . . . . dormit.
5 Metella in ātriō . . . . . .
6 . . . . . in triclīniō cēnat.

2 Complete each sentence with a word that makes good sense, choosing your answer from the words in parentheses. Write out the completed sentence in Latin, and then translate it into English.

for example: amīcus Caecilium . . . . . . (sedet, vīsitat)
     amīcus Caecilium vīsitat.
     A friend visits Caecilius.

1 Caecilius pecūniam . . . . . . (numerat, dormit)
2 Clēmēns vīnum . . . . . . (labōrat, portat)
3 ancilla hortum . . . . . . (intrat, gustat)
4 Metella mercātōrem . . . . . . (salūtat, cantat)
5 Quīntus cēnam . . . . . . (vīsitat, cōnsūmit)
6 servus vīllam . . . . . . (dormit, intrat, portat)
7 amīcus Grumiōnem . . . . . . (spectat, stat, recumbit)
8 māter fīlium . . . . . . (surgit, dormit, vituperat)
9 mercātor canem . . . . . . (sedet, cōnsūmit, audit)
10 dominus ancillam . . . . . . (scrībit, laudat, numerat)

3 Translate into English:

amīcus Grumiōnem vīsitat. amīcus est servus. servus vīllam intrat. Clēmēns est in ātriō. servus Clēmentem videt. Clēmēns servum salūtat. servus culīnam intrat. servus culīnam circumspectat.

Grumiō nōn est in culīnā. servus cibum videt. cibus est parātus! servus cibum gustat. cibus est optimus. 5

Grumiō culīnam intrat. Grumiō amīcum videt. amīcus cibum cōnsūmit! coquus est īrātus.

"pestis! furcifer!" coquus clāmat. coquus amīcum vituperat.

parātus *ready*

Food excavated at Pompeii: walnuts (top), a loaf (bottom), grain (right)

Two views from the House of the Vettii: the garden (above) and kitchen stove (below)

Daily Life

The day began early for Caecilius and the members of his household. He would usually get up at dawn. His slaves were up even earlier, sweeping and dusting and polishing. Caecilius did not spend much time dressing. The first garment that he put on was his tunic, similar to a short-sleeved shirt, then his toga, which was a large woolen cloak arranged in complicated folds, and finally his shoes, which were rather like modern sandals. A quick wash of the hands and face with cold water was enough at that time of the morning; later he would visit a barber to be shaved; and in the afternoon he would take a long, leisurely bath.

His wife, Metella, also got up early. With the help of a skilled slave-woman, she did her hair in the latest style, put on her make-up, including powder, rouge, and mascara, and arranged her jewelry, of which she had a large and varied collection.

Breakfast was only a light snack. It was often no more than a cup of water and a piece of bread. The first duty of the day for Caecilius was to receive the respectful greetings of a number of poorer people and freedmen who had previously been his slaves. To these visitors he distributed small sums of money, and, if they were in any kind of trouble, he gave them as much help and protection as he could. In return they helped Caecilius in several ways; for example, they accompanied him as a group of supporters on public occasions, and they might also be employed by him in business affairs. They were known as his **clientēs** and he was their **patrōnus**. When Caecilius had finished seeing his clientes, he set out for the **forum**, or business center, where he spent the rest of the morning trading and banking.

Lunch was eaten at noon and this also was a light meal. It usually consisted of some meat or fish followed by fruit. Business ended soon after lunch. Caecilius would then have a short siesta before going to the baths. Towards the end of the afternoon, the main meal of the day began. This was called **cēna**.

During the winter Caecilius used the inner dining-room near the atrium; but in the summer he would generally have preferred the dining-room at the back of the house which faced out onto the garden. Three couches were arranged around a circular table. This dining-table, though small, was very elegantly carved and decorated. Each couch had

The arrows show the position of the people eating dinner.

A dining-room

places for three people. The diners reclined on these couches, leaning on their left elbow and taking food from the table with their right hand. The food was cut up by a slave before being served, and the diners ate it with their fingers or a spoon. Forks were not used by the Romans. Not all Romans reclined when eating dinner, but it was usual among rich or upper-class families; poor people, slaves, and children would eat sitting up.

The meal began with a first course of light dishes to whet the appetite. Eggs and fish were often served. Then came the main course, in which a variety of meat dishes would be offered. Beef, pork, mutton, and poultry were all popular, and in preparing them the cook would do his best to show off his skill and imagination. Finally, the dessert was brought in, consisting of fruit and cheese. Wine produced locally from the vineyards on Vesuvius was drunk throughout the meal. There was no hurry, for this was the big social occasion of the day. With much talk and laughter, with music and singing, the exchange of gossip and drinking of toasts, dinner sometimes went on until late in the evening.

Words and Phrases Checklist

You have now met the following words three times or more. Check that you are able to translate them.

amīcus	*friend*
ancilla	*slave-girl, slave-woman*
cēna	*dinner*
cibus	*food*
dominus	*master*
dormit	*sleeps*
gustat	*tastes*
intrat	*enters*
laetus	*happy*
laudat	*praises*
mēnsa	*table*
mercātor	*merchant*
quoque	*also, too*
salūtat	*greets*

Word Search

Match each definition with one of the words given below.

amicable, ancillary, commerce, disgust, domination, dormitory, laudable

1 . . . . . : to offend or sicken
2 . . . . . : trade
3 . . . . . : friendly
4 . . . . . : worthy of praise
5 . . . . . : helpful; additional
6 . . . . . : power or control
7 . . . . . : sleeping quarters

Pantagathus, Celer, Syphāx

in forō

Caecilius nōn est in vīllā. Caecilius in forō labōrat. Caecilius est argentārius. argentārius pecūniam numerat.

Caecilius forum circumspectat. ecce! pictor in forō ambulat. pictor est Celer. Celer Caecilium salūtat.

ecce! tōnsor quoque est in forō. tōnsor est Pantagathus. Caecilius tōnsōrem videt.   5

"salvē!" Caecilius tōnsōrem salūtat.

"salvē!" Pantagathus respondet.

ecce! vēnālīcius forum intrat. vēnālīcius est Syphāx. vēnālīcius mercātōrem exspectat. mercātor nōn venit. Syphāx est īrātus.   10
Syphāx mercātōrem vituperat.

Words and Phrases

in forō	*in the forum*	tōnsor	*barber*
ecce!	*see! look!*	vēnālīcius	*slave-dealer*
pictor	*painter, artist*	nōn venit	*does not come*
ambulat	*is walking*		

Table of weights and measures from the forum in Pompeii

pictor

pictor ad vīllam venit. pictor est Celer. Celer iānuam pulsat.
Clēmēns pictōrem nōn audit. servus est in hortō. Celer clāmat. canis
Celerem audit et lātrat. Quīntus canem audit. Quīntus ad iānuam
venit. fīlius iānuam aperit. Celer Quīntum salūtat et vīllam intrat.

Metella est in culīnā. Quīntus mātrem vocat. Metella ātrium   5
intrat. pictor Metellam salūtat. Metella pictōrem ad triclīnium
dūcit.

Celer in triclīniō labōrat. Celer pictūram pingit. magnus leō est in
pictūrā. Herculēs quoque est in pictūrā. leō Herculem ferōciter
petit. Herculēs magnum fūstem tenet et leōnem verberat. Herculēs   10
est fortis.

Caecilius ad vīllam revenit et triclīnium intrat. Caecilius
pictūram intentē spectat et pictūram laudat.

Words and Phrases

ad vīllam	*to the house*	ferōciter	*fiercely*
iānuam pulsat	*knocks on the door*	petit	*heads for, attacks*
ad iānuam	*to the door*	fūstem	*club*
aperit	*opens*	tenet	*is holding*
vocat	*calls*	verberat	*is striking*
dūcit	*leads*	fortis	*brave*
pictūram pingit/	*paints a picture*	revenit	*returns*
magnus	*big, large*	intentē	*intently*
leō	*lion*		

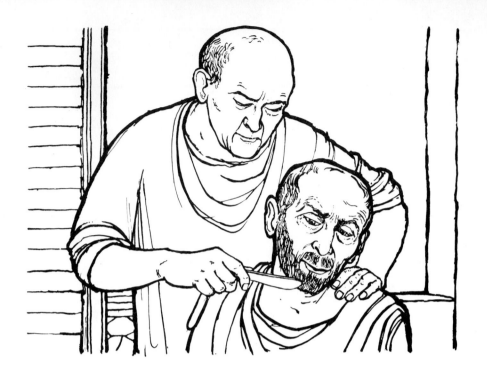

When you have read this story, answer the questions at the end.

tōnsor

tōnsor in tabernā labōrat. tōnsor est Pantagathus. Caecilius intrat.

    "salvē, tōnsor!" inquit Caecilius.

    "salvē!" respondet Pantagathus.

    tōnsor est occupātus. senex in sellā sedet. Pantagathus
novāculam tenet et barbam tondet. senex novāculam intentē   5
spectat.

    poēta tabernam intrat. poēta in tabernā stat et versum recitat.
Caecilius rīdet, sed tōnsor nōn rīdet. versus est scurrīlis; tōnsor est
īrātus.

    "furcifer! furcifer!" clāmat Pantagathus. senex est perterritus.   10
tōnsor barbam nōn tondet. tōnsor senem secat. multus sanguis fluit.

    Caecilius surgit et ē tabernā exit.

Barber's shears

Words and Phrases

in tabernā	*in the shop*	versum recitat	*recites a line, recites a verse*
inquit	*says*	rīdet	*laughs, smiles*
occupātus	*busy*	sed	*but*
senex	*old man*	scurrīlis	*obscene, dirty*
in sellā	*in the chair*	perterritus	*terrified*
novāculam	*razor*	secat	*cuts*
barbam tondet	*is trimming his beard*	multus	*much*
		sanguis fluit	*blood flows*
poēta	*poet*	ē tabernā	*out of the shop*

Questions

1 Who is working in the shop when Caecilius arrives? What is he doing?
2 Who comes into the shop after Caecilius? What does he do?
3 Why is the barber angry?
4 What happens to the old man?
5 What does Caecilius do? Why?

vēnālīcius

Caecilius ad portum ambulat. Caecilius portum circumspectat.
argentārius nāvem Syriam videt, et ad nāvem ambulat. Syphāx
prope nāvem stat.

"salvē, Syphāx!" clāmat argentārius. Syphāx est vēnālīcius.
Syphāx Caecilium salūtat.   5

Caecilius servum quaerit. Syphāx rīdet. ecce! Syphāx magnum
servum habet. Caecilius servum spectat. argentārius nōn est
contentus. argentārius servum nōn emit.

"vīnum!" clāmat Syphāx. ancilla vīnum ad Caecilium portat.
argentārius vīnum bibit.   10

Caecilius ancillam spectat. ancilla est pulchra. ancilla rīdet.
ancilla Caecilium dēlectat. vēnālīcius quoque rīdet.

"Melissa cēnam optimam coquit," inquit vēnālīcius. "Melissa
linguam Latīnam discit. Melissa est docta et pulchra. Melissa . . ."

"satis! satis!" clāmat Caecilius. Caecilius Melissam emit et ad   15
vīllam revenit. Melissa Grumiōnem dēlectat. Melissa Quīntum
dēlectat. ēheu! ancilla Metellam nōn dēlectat.

Words and Phrases

ad portum	*to the harbor*	emit	*buys*
nāvem	*ship*	pulchra	*beautiful*
prope nāvem	*near the ship*	linguam	*language*
quaerit	*is searching for,*	discit	*is learning*
	is looking for	docta	*skillful, good at her job*
habet	*has*	satis	*enough*
contentus	*satisfied*	ēheu!	*alas! oh dear!*

Names and Proper Adjectives

Syriam	*Syrian*	Latīnam	*Latin*

About the Language

1 Notice the difference between the nominative case and the accusative case of the following words:

NOMINATIVE	Metella	Caecilius	mercātor
ACCUSATIVE	Metellam	Caecilium	mercātōrem

2 A large number of words, such as **ancilla** and **taberna**, form their accusative in the same way as **Metella**. They are known as the *first declension,* and look like this:

NOMINATIVE	Metella	ancilla	taberna
ACCUSATIVE	Metellam	ancillam	tabernam

3 Another large group of words is known as the *second declension.* Most of these words form their accusative in the same way as **Caecilius**. For example:

NOMINATIVE	Caecilius	servus	amīcus
ACCUSATIVE	Caecilium	servum	amīcum

4 You have also met several words belonging to the *third declension.* For example:

NOMINATIVE	mercātor	leō	senex
ACCUSATIVE	mercātōrem	leōnem	senem

The nominative of the third declension may take various forms; but the accusative nearly always ends in **-em**.

Practicing the Language

1 Complete each sentence with a word that makes good sense, choosing your answer from the words in parentheses. Write out the completed sentence in Latin, and then translate it into English.

1 mercātor ē vīllā . . . . . . (quaerit, ambulat)
2 servus ad hortum . . . . . . (recitat, venit)
3 coquus ad culīnam . . . . . . (revenit, habet)
4 Syphāx servum ad vīllam . . . . . . (dūcit, ambulat)
5 Clēmēns cibum ad Caecilium . . . . . . (salit, venit, portat)

2 Complete each sentence with the right word, choosing your answer from the words in parentheses. Write out the completed sentence in Latin, and then translate it into English.

for example: . . . . . . vīnum portat. (servus, servum)
               servus vīnum portat.
               The slave carries the wine.

1 amīcus . . . . . laudat. (servus, servum)
2 senex . . . . . intrat. (taberna, tabernam)
3 . . . . . cibum gustat. (dominus, dominum)
4 . . . . . Metellam salūtat. (mercātor, mercātōrem)
5 vēnālīcius . . . . . videt. (tōnsor, tōnsōrem)
6 . . . . . versum recitat. (poēta, poētam)
7 . . . . . in forō ambulat. (senex, senem)
8 ancilla . . . . . ad ātrium dūcit. (pictor, pictōrem)

Intersection of two streets in Pompeii

The Town of Pompeii

The town of Pompeii was built on a low hill of volcanic rock about five miles (eight kilometers) south of Mount Vesuvius and close to the mouth of a small river. It was one of a number of prosperous towns in the fertile region of Campania. Outside the towns, especially along the coast of the bay, were many villas and farming estates, often owned by wealthy Romans, who were attracted to this area by its pleasant climate and peaceful surroundings.

The town itself covered 163 acres (66 hectares), and was surrounded by a wall. The wall had eleven towers and eight gates. Roads led out from these gates to the neighboring towns of Herculaneum, Nola, Nuceria, Stabiae, and to the harbor. Two wide main streets, known today as the Street of Shops and Stabiae Street, crossed near the center of the town; a third main street ran parallel to the Street of Shops.

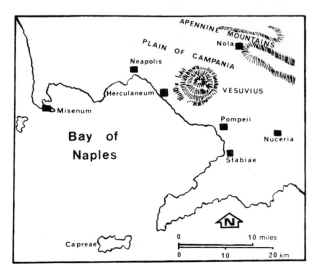

Campania and the Bay of Naples

The other streets, most of them also running in straight lines, divided the town neatly into blocks. There is no evidence that the Pompeians used street names and a stranger visiting the town would have had to ask his way from the local people.

The streets, constructed of volcanic stone, had high sidewalks on one or both sides to enable pedestrians to keep out of the garbage and avoid the traffic of wagons, horses, and mules. Stepping-stones provided convenient crossing places. Public water fountains stood at many street corners. The town's water supply was brought from the hills by an aqueduct; on reaching Pompeii it was stored in large tanks on high ground at the northern side. The pressure created by the water in these tanks provided a good flow through underground lead pipes to all parts of the town, including the three sets of public baths. Although most people drew their water from the public fountains, the wealthier citizens paid special rates which allowed them to take a private supply from the public pipes straight into their homes.

In all the main streets there were bakers' stores and bars where hot and cold drinks and snacks could be bought. The main shopping areas were in the forum, and along the Street of Shops northeast of the Stabian baths.

Carved or painted signs indicated different kinds of stores. A figure of a goat announced a dairy (see p.44); a hammer and chisel, a stonemason. General advertisements and public notices were painted on the whitewashed walls outside stores and houses. We can still see notices advertising shows in the amphitheater and political slogans supporting candidates at the last election.

At the western end of the town was the forum. This large open space, with a covered colonnade on three sides, was the center for business and local government.

There were two theaters. Popular shows for large audiences were performed in the big open-air theater, which could hold about 5,000 people, while the smaller one, which was roofed, was used for concerts

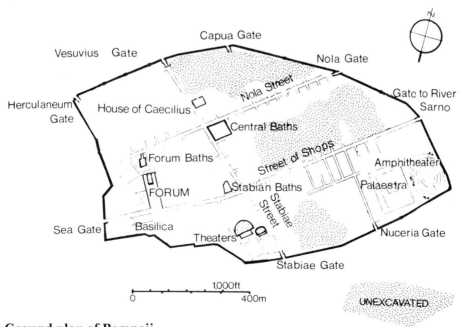

Ground plan of Pompeii

and for other shows. At the eastern end of the town was a huge sports field or **palaestra**, and next to it an amphitheater in which gladiatorial combats and wild-animal hunts were staged. This amphitheater was large enough to seat every inhabitant in Pompeii and visitors from neighboring towns as well.

Like a modern seaport, Pompeii was a place where people of many nationalities were to be seen: Romans, Greeks, Syrians, Jews, Africans, Spaniards, and probably several other nationalities as well, with their different languages and different religions. This regular coming and going of people, many of whom were merchants and businessmen, was made possible by the peaceful conditions that existed throughout the Roman empire at this time.

From Britain in the northwest to Syria and Palestine in the east, Rome maintained peace and provided firm government. The frontiers of the empire were held secure by Roman troops stationed at important points. Travel was made easy by a system of well-built roads; ships carried foodstuffs and luxury goods across the Mediterranean; taxes were collected in the provinces and the wealth of Rome increased. Pompeii was only a medium-sized town but played its part in the flourishing commercial life of the empire.

Store sign for a dairy

North entrance to the forum in Pompeii

Words and Phrases Checklist

You have now met the following words three times or more. Check that you are able to translate them.

ad	*to*	nāvis	*ship*
bibit	*drinks*	nōn	*not*
circumspectat	*looks around*	portat	*carries*
clāmat	*shouts*	respondet	*replies*
ecce!	*see! look!*	rīdet	*laughs, smiles*
et	*and*	salvē!	*hello!*
exit	*goes out*	surgit	*gets up, rises*
exspectat	*waits for*	taberna	*store, shop* (also *inn* in
forum	*forum, business center*		other contexts)
iānua	*door*	videt	*sees*
īrātus	*angry*	vīlla	*house*
leō	*lion*	vīnum	*wine*
magnus	*big, large, great*		

Word Search

Match each definition with one of the words given below.

imbibe, irate, magnitude, naval, portable, ridicule, surge

1 . . . . . : pertaining to ships or sailing
2 . . . . . : enraged
3 . . . . . : greatness or extent
4 . . . . . : capable of being carried
5 . . . . . : to rise; to swell
6 . . . . . : to drink
7 . . . . . : to make fun of

Stage 4

in forō

Grumiō: ego sum coquus.
      ego cēnam coquō.

Caecilius: ego sum argentārius.
      ego pecūniam habeō.

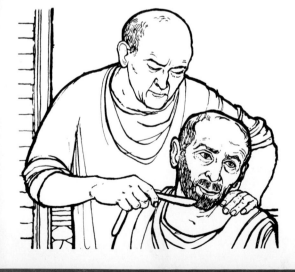

Pantagathus: ego sum tōnsor.
      ego barbam
      tondeō.

Syphāx: ego sum vēnālīcius.
ego servum vēndō.

poēta: ego sum poēta.
ego versum recitō.

Celer: ego sum pictor.
ego leōnem pingō.

Quīntus: quid tū coquis?
Grumiō: ego cēnam coquō.

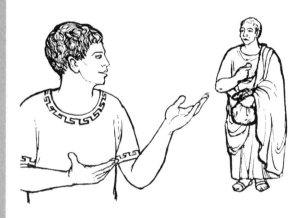

Quīntus: quid tū habēs?
mercātor: ego pecūniam
habeō.

Quīntus: quid tū tondēs?
tōnsor: ego barbam tondeō.

Quīntus: quid tū vēndis?
vēnālīcius: ego servum
vēndō.

Quīntus: quid tū recitās?
poēta: ego versum recitō.

Quīntus: quid tū pingis?
pictor: ego leōnem pingō.

Metella: quis es tū?
ancilla: ego sum Melissa.

Metella: quis es tū?
vēnālīcius: ego sum Syphāx.

Metella: quis es tū?
servus: ego sum Clēmēns.

**Meeting hall of the cloth merchants
(sponsored by Eumachia):
facade of building (above),
statue of Eumachia (below)**

Hermogenēs

Caecilius est in forō. Caecilius in forō argentāriam habet. Hermogenēs ad forum venit. Hermogenēs est mercātor Graecus. mercātor Caecilium salūtat.

"ego sum mercātor Graecus," inquit Hermogenēs. "ego sum mercātor probus. ego pecūniam quaerō." 5

"cūr tū pecūniam quaeris?" inquit Caecilius.

"ego nāvem habeō," respondet Hermogenēs. "sed nāvis nōn adest; nāvis est in Graeciā. ego tamen sum probus. ego semper pecūniam reddō." *however*

"ecce!" inquit Caecilius. "ego cēram habeō. tū ānulum habēs?" 10

"ego ānulum habeō," respondet Hermogenēs. "ānulus signum habet. ecce! ego signum in cērā imprimō."

Caecilius pecūniam trādit. mercātor pecūniam capit et ē forō currit.

ēheu! Hermogenēs nōn revenit. mercātor pecūniam nōn reddit. 15 Caecilius Hermogenem ad basilicam vocat.

Words and Phrases

argentāriam	*banker's stall*
probus	*honest*
cūr?	*why?*
nōn adest	*is not here*
tamen	*however*
semper	*always*
cēram	*wax tablet*
ego . . . reddō	*I give back*
ānulum	*ring*
signum	*seal, sign*
ego . . . imprimō	*I press*
trādit	*hands over*
capit	*takes*
currit	*runs*
ad basilicam	*to court*

Names and Proper Adjectives

Graecus	*Greek*
in Graeciā	*in Greece*

in basilicā

iūdex basilicam intrat.

iūdex:	quis es tū?
Caecilius:	ego sum Lūcius Caecilius Iūcundus.
iūdex:	tū es Pompēiānus?
Caecilius:	ego sum Pompēiānus.
iūdex:	quid tū in urbe agis?
Caecilius:	ego cotīdiē ad forum veniō. ego sum argentārius.
iūdex:	cūr tū hodiē ad basilicam venīs?
Caecilius:	Hermogenēs multam pecūniam dēbet. Hermogenēs
	pecūniam nōn reddit.
Hermogenēs:	Caecilius est mendāx!
iūdex:	quis es tū?
Hermogenēs:	ego sum Hermogenēs.
iūdex:	Hermogenēs, quid tū in urbe agis?
Hermogenēs:	ego in forō negōtium agō. ego sum mercātor.
iūdex:	quid tū respondēs? tū pecūniam dēbēs?
Hermogenēs:	ego pecūniam nōn dēbeō. amīcus meus est testis.
amīcus:	ego sum testis. Hermogenēs pecūniam nōn dēbet.
	Caecilius est mendāx.

Line numbers: 5, 10, 15

Words and Phrases

iūdex	*judge*
quis?	*who?*
quid tū . . . agis?	*what do you do?*
in urbe	*in the city*
cotīdiē	*every day*
hodiē	*today*
dēbet	*owes*
mendāx	*liar*
ego . . . negōtium agō	*I work, I do business*
meus	*my, mine*
testis	*witness*

Names and Proper Adjectives

Pompēiānus   *Pompeian, citizen of Pompeii*

Caecilius:	tū, Hermogenēs, es mendāx. amīcus tuus quoque est	20
	mendāx. tū pecūniam nōn reddis . . . *thing rrt*	
iūdex:	satis! tū Hermogenem accūsās, sed tū rem nōn	
	probās.	
Caecilius:	ego cēram habeō. tū signum in cērā vidēs.	
Hermogenēs:	ēheu!	25
iūdex:	Hermogenēs, tū ānulum habēs?	
Caecilius:	ecce! Hermogenēs ānulum cēlat.	
iūdex:	ubi est ānulus? ecce! ānulus rem probat. ego	
	Hermogenem convincō.	

Words and Phrases

tuus	*your*
tū accūsās	*you accuse*
tū rem nōn probās	*you do not prove the case*
cēlat	*is hiding*
ubi?	*where?*
ego convincō	*I convict, I find guilty*

The basilica at Pompeii

About the Language

1 In the first three Stages, you met sentences like this:

servus currit.   *The slave runs.*
ancilla ambulat.   *The slave-girl walks.*
mercātor sedet.   *The merchant sits.*

2 In Stage 4, you have met sentences with *I* and *you*:

ego currō.   *I run.*   tū curris.   *You run.*
ego ambulō.   *I walk.*   tū ambulās.   *You walk.*
ego sedeō.   *I sit.*   tū sedēs.   *You sit.*

3 Notice the three different forms of each word:

ego currō.   tū curris.   servus currit.
ego ambulō.   tū ambulās.   ancilla ambulat.
ego sedeō.   tū sedēs.   mercātor sedet.

Notice also that the words **ego** and **tū** are not strictly necessary, since the endings **-ō** and **-s** make it clear that *I* and *you* are being spoken about. The Romans usually left out **ego** and **tū**, unless they wanted to emphasize that they meant *I* or *you*.

4 The following example is rather different:

ego sum īrātus.   *I am angry.*
tū es īrātus.   *You are angry.*
servus est īrātus.   *The slave is angry.*

5 Study and translate the following sentences:

1 Caecilius recitat. ego recitō.
2 Quīntus dormit. tū dormīs.
3 tū labōrās. servus labōrat.
4 Syphāx servum habet. ego servum habeō.
5 ego pecūniam trādō. tū pecūniam trādis.
6 Pantagathus est tōnsor. tū es mercātor. ego sum poēta.
7 ambulō; circumspectō; circumspectās.
8 audiō; audīs; habēs.

Practicing the Language

1 Complete each pair of sentences with a suitable word, choosing your answer from the words in parentheses, and then translate them into English.

for example: ego sum argentārius.
              ego pecūniam . . . . . . (habeō, salūtō)

              ego sum argentārius.
              ego pecūniam habeō.

              I am a banker.
              I have money.

1 ego sum mercātor.
   ego nāvem . . . . . .(stō, habeō)
2 ego sum coquus.
   ego cēnam . . . . . .(dormiō, coquō)
3 ego sum Herculēs.
   ego fūstem . . . . . .(teneō, sedeō)
4 ego sum servus.
   ego in culīnā . . . . . .(habeō, labōrō)
5 tū es amīcus.
   tū vīllam . . . . . .(intrās, dūcis)
6 tū es ancilla.
   tū suāviter . . . . . . (venīs, cantās)
7 tū es mendāx.
   tū pecūniam . . . . . . (dēbēs, ambulās)
8 tū es iūdex.
   tū Hermogenem . . . . . . (curris, convincis)
9 ego sum Syphāx.
   ego ancillam . . . . . . (vēndō, ambulō)
10 tū es senex.
   tū in tabernā . . . . . . (tenēs, sedēs)

2 Translate into English:

Celer in vīllā labōrat. Celer pictūram in triclīniō pingit. magnus leō est in pictūrā. Celer ē vīllā discēdit.

Grumiō ē tabernā revenit et vīllam intrat. Grumiō est ēbrius. Grumiō pictūram videt. Grumiō est perterritus.

"ēheu!" inquit Grumiō. "leō est in triclīniō. leō mē spectat. leō   5
mē ferōciter petit."

Grumiō ē triclīniō currit et culīnam intrat. Clēmēns est in culīnā. Clēmēns Grumiōnem spectat.

"cūr tū es perterritus?" inquit Clēmēns.

"ēheu! leō est in triclīniō," inquit Grumiō.   10

"ita vērō," respondet Clēmēns, "et servus ēbrius est in culīnā."

discēdit	*departs, leaves*
ē tabernā	*from the inn*
ēbrius	*drunk*
ita vērō	*yes*

The Forum

The forum was the civic center and the heart of the business life of Pompeii. It was a large open space surrounded on three sides by a colonnade, with various important public buildings grouped closely around it. The open area, 156 yards (143 meters) long and 42 yards (38 meters) wide, was paved with stone. In it stood a number of statues commemorating the emperor, members of the emperor's family, and local citizens who had given distinguished service to the town.

The illustration on page 60 shows a typical scene in the forum. The merchant on the left has set up his wooden stall and is selling small articles of ironware, pincers, knives, and hammers; the merchant on the right is a shoemaker. He has seated his customers on stools while he shows them his goods. Behind the merchants is the colonnade. This elegant structure, supported by columns of white marble, provided an open corridor in which people could walk and do business out of the heat of the sun in the summer and protected from the rain in winter.

On the right of the drawing are two statues of important citizens mounted on horseback. Behind them is one of the bronze gates through which people entered the forum. Wheeled traffic was not allowed to enter this commercial area. The whole forum was a pedestrian precinct, and a row of upright stones at each entrance made an effective barrier.

Merchant's scales

Relief showing a food store. Note that the storekeeper is a woman. The wickerwork cage is probably for poultry. The monkeys may also have been for sale as food.

Street of Shops

In the drawing above, you see a public bulletin board fixed across the pedestals of three statues, and two people studying the bulletins. There were no newspapers in Pompeii, but certain kinds of information, such as election results and dates of processions and shows, had to be publicized. This was done by painting bulletins on the outside walls of various buildings and by putting up bulletin boards in the forum.

In addition to official announcements, thousands of casual scribblings were made on the walls by ordinary people recording lost property, space for rent, lovers' messages, and smart remarks. One of these advertisements says,

"A bronze jar has been lost from this shop. A reward is offered for its recovery."

Another complains of noise at night and asks the **aedile** (the official who was responsible for law and order) to do something about it:

"Macerior requests the aedile to stop people from making a noise in the streets and disturbing decent folk who are asleep."

Some of the most important public buildings were situated around the forum. In a prominent position at the north end stood the temple of Jupiter, the greatest of the Roman gods. The temple of Apollo lay just to the south, and nearby was a public weights and measures table. Not far off was the speakers' platform (**tribūnal**), from which important speeches and announcements were made. At the southwest corner stood the **basilica**, or court building. This was a large, long building with rows of pillars inside and a high platform at one end on which the two senior officials, called **duovirī**, sat when hearing lawsuits. The basilica was also

Ground plan of the forum

1 Temple of Jupiter
2 Temple of Apollo
3 Basilica
4 Temple of Venus
5 Offices
6 Statues
7 Meeting hall of the
   cloth merchants
8 Temple of the emperors
9 Temple of the lares of
   Pompeii
10 Market hall
11 Baths
12 Tribunal

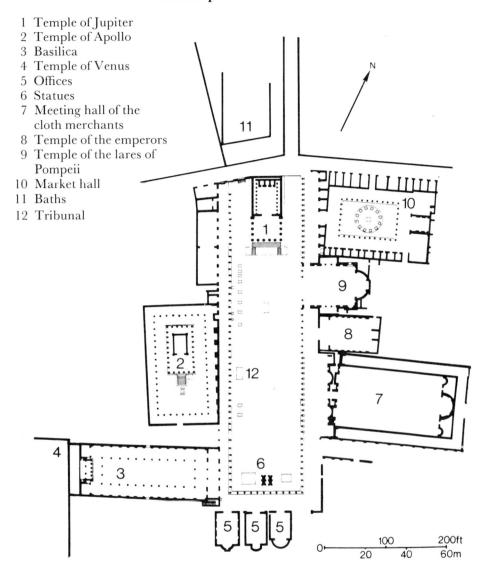

used as a meeting place for businessmen. Southwest of the basilica was the temple of Venus, an important goddess for the Pompeians, who believed she took a special interest in their town.

Along the south side of the forum were three offices in which the town governing board conducted its business. On the east side was the meeting hall of the cloth merchants. As this was one of the most prosperous industries in the town, it is not surprising that its headquarters were large and occupied such a prominent site. Next to it stood a temple in honor of the Roman emperors, and by the side of that a temple dedicated to the **larēs**, or guardian spirits of Pompeii. We have now mentioned five religious shrines around or near the forum. There were many others elsewhere in the town, including a temple of Isis, an Egyptian goddess, whose worship had been brought to Italy. In addition to these public shrines, each home had its own gods, called the "lares and penates." It is not easy for us to understand clearly the beliefs of the Pompeians about their gods, but perhaps the first point to keep in mind is that it seemed to them quite natural to believe in many gods rather than one. Different gods cared for different parts of human life. Apollo, for example, was concerned with law, medicine, and music; Venus was the goddess of love and beauty.

In the northeast corner of the forum was a large covered market which contained permanent stores rather than temporary stalls. The merchants here sold mainly meat, fish, and vegetables. Northwest of the market, just behind the temple of Jupiter, stood a set of public baths.

Business, religion, local government: these were the official purposes of the forum and its surrounding buildings. This great crowded square was the center of much of the open-air life in Pompeii. Here people gathered to do business, to shop, or just to stroll and gossip with their friends.

Speakers' platform (the tribunal) in the forum at Pompeii

Narrow street in Pompeii

Words and Phrases Checklist

agit	*does*
negōtium agit	*does business, works*
ānulus	*ring*
cēra	*wax, wax tablet*
coquit	*cooks*
cūr?	*why?*
ē	*out of, from*
ego	*I*
ēheu!	*alas! oh dear!*
habet	*has*
inquit	*says*
iūdex	*judge*
mendāx	*liar*
pecūnia	*money*
perterritus	*terrified*
poēta	*poet*
quaerit	*searches for, looks for*
quis?	*who?*
reddit	*gives back*
satis	*enough*
sed	*but*
signum	*sign, seal* (also *signal* in other contexts)
tū	*you*
vēndit	*sells*
vocat	*calls*

Word Search

Match each definition with one of the words given below.

advocate, agent, impecunious, judicial, satisfy, terrify, vendor

1 . . . . . : to fulfill
2 . . . . . : a person who sells something
3 . . . . . : a defender or supporter
4 . . . . . : pertaining to legal practice
5 . . . . . : a person who acts on another's behalf
6 . . . . . : to frighten
7 . . . . . : having little money, poor

in theātrō

in viā

canis est in viā.

canēs sunt in viā.

servus est in viā.

servī sunt in viā.

puella est in viā.

puellae sunt in viā.

puer est in viā.

puerī sunt in viā.

mercātor est in viā.

mercātōrēs sunt in viā.

in theātrō

spectātor in theātrō sedet.

spectātōrēs in theātrō sedent.

āctor in scaenā stat.

āctōrēs in scaenā stant.

fēmina spectat.

fēminae spectant.

senex dormit.

senēs dormiunt.

iuvenis plaudit.

iuvenēs plaudunt.

āctōrēs

magna turba est in urbe. fēminae et puellae sunt in turbā. senēs
quoque et iuvenēs sunt in turbā. servī hodiē nōn labōrant. senēs
hodiē nōn dormiunt. mercātōrēs hodiē nōn sunt occupātī.
Pompēiānī sunt ōtiōsī. urbs tamen nōn est quiēta. Pompēiānī ad
theātrum contendunt. magnus clāmor est in urbe.   5

    agricolae urbem intrant. nautae urbem petunt. pāstōrēs dē monte
veniunt et ad urbem contendunt. turba per portam ruit.

    nūntius in forō clāmat: "āctōrēs sunt in urbe. āctōrēs sunt in
theātrō. Priscus fābulam dat. Priscus fābulam optimam dat. āctōrēs
sunt Actius et Sorex."   10

    Caecilius et Metella ē vīllā discēdunt. argentārius et uxor ad
theātrum ambulant. Clēmēns et Melissa ad theātrum contendunt.
sed Grumiō in vīllā manet.

Words and Phrases

āctōrēs	*actors*	nautae	*sailors*
turba	*crowd*	petunt	*head for, seek*
fēminae	*women*	pāstōrēs	*shepherds*
puellae	*girls*	dē monte	*down from the mountain*
iuvenēs	*young men*	per portam	*through the gate*
ōtiōsī	*at leisure, with time off, idle*	ruit	*rushes*
quiēta	*quiet*	nūntius	*messenger*
ad theātrum	*to the theater*	fābulam dat	*is putting on a play*
contendunt	*hurry*	uxor	*wife*
clāmor	*shout, uproar*	manet	*remains, stays*
agricolae	*farmers*		

Mosaic showing a musical interlude in a play

Poppaea

Poppaea est ancilla. ancilla prope iānuam stat. ancilla viam spectat. dominus (Near)
in hortō dormit. dominus est Lucriō. Lucriō est senex.

Poppaea: ego amīcum meum exspectō. ubi est amīcus?
    (Lucriō stertit.)
    ēheu! Lucriō est in vīllā.   street short   5
    (agricolae in viā clāmant.)

agricolae: euge! agricolae hodiē nōn labōrant!

Poppaea: Lucriō! Lucriō! agricolae urbem intrant. agricolae
    adsunt.

Words and Phrases

euge!	*hurrah!*
adsunt	*are here*

Lucriō: (*sēmisomnus*) a . . . a . . . agricolae?   10
puerī: euge! Sorex! Actius! āctōrēs adsunt.
Poppaea: Lucriō! Lucriō! puerī per viam currunt.
Lucriō: quid tū clāmās, Poppaea? cūr tū clāmōrem facis?
Poppaea: Lucriō, Pompēiānī clāmōrem faciunt. agricolae et puerī
            sunt in viā.   15
Lucriō: cūr tū mē vexās?
Poppaea: āctōrēs in theātrō fābulam agunt.
Lucriō: āctōrēs?
Poppaea: Sorex et Actius adsunt.
Lucriō: quid tū dīcis?   20
Poppaea: (*īrāta*) senēs ad theātrum ambulant, iuvenēs ad theātrum
            contendunt, omnēs Pompēiānī ad theātrum ruunt.
            āctōrēs in theātrō fābulam agunt.
Lucriō: euge! āctōrēs adsunt. ego quoque ad theātrum contendō.
            (*exit Lucriō. amīcus vīllam intrat.*)   25
amīcus: salvē! mea columba!
Poppaea: Grumiō, dēliciae meae! salvē!
Grumiō: ubi est dominus tuus?
Poppaea: Lucriō abest.
Grumiō: euge!   30

Words and Phrases

sēmisomnus	*half-asleep*
puerī	*boys*
tū clāmōrem facis	*you make a noise*
tū . . . vexās	*you annoy*
fābulam agunt	*act in a play*
tū dīcis	*you say*
omnēs	*all*
mea columba	*my dove*
dēliciae meae	*my darling*
abest	*is out*

About the Language

1 In the first four Stages, you have met sentences like these:

servus labōrat.   leō currit.
The slave works.   *The lion runs.*

puella sedet.   mercātor dormit.
The girl sits.   *The merchant sleeps.*

Sentences like these refer to *one* person or thing, and the form of the words is said to be *singular*.

2 Sentences which refer to *more* than one person or thing use a different form of the words, known as the *plural*. Compare the singular and plural forms in the following sentences:

SINGULAR   PLURAL
servus labōrat.   servī labōrant.
The slave works.   *The slaves work.*

puella sedet.   puellae sedent.
The girl sits.   *The girls sit.*

leō currit.   leōnēs currunt.
The lion runs.   *The lions run.*

mercātor dormit.   mercātōrēs dormiunt.
The merchant sleeps.   *The merchants sleep.*

Notice that in each of these sentences *both* words show the difference between singular and plural.

3 Study and translate the following sentences:

1 amīcus ambulat. amīcī ambulant.
2 āctor clāmat. āctōrēs clāmant.
3 senēs dormiunt. senex dormit.
4 vēnālīciī intrant. vēnālīcius intrat.
5 ancilla respondet. ancillae respondent.

4 Notice the difference between *is* and *are* in Latin:

mercātor est in viā.   mercātōrēs sunt in viā.
The merchant is in the street.   *The merchants are in the street.*

Practicing the Language

1 Complete each sentence with the right word. Write out the completed sentence in Latin, and then translate it.

for example: senēs . . . . . . (dormit, dormiunt)
                senēs dormiunt.
                The old men are sleeping.

1 āctōrēs . . . . . . (adest, adsunt)
2 puellae in theātrō . . . . . . (sedent, sedet)
3 agricolae ad urbem . . . . . . (currunt, currit)
4 Pompēiānī clāmōrem . . . . . . (facit, faciunt)
5 servī ad theātrum . . . . . . (contendit, contendunt)

2 Complete each sentence with the right word. Write out the completed sentence in Latin, and then translate it.

for example: mercātōrēs Caecilium . . . . . . (quaerit, quaerunt)
                mercātōrēs Caecilium quaerunt.
                The merchants are looking for Caecilius.

1 pāstōrēs ad theātrum . . . . . . (contendit, contendunt)
2 pāstor pecūniam nōn . . . . . . (habet, habent)
3 puella āctōrem . . . . . . (laudat, laudant)
4 fēminae fābulam . . . . . . (spectat, spectant)
5 vēnālīciī ad urbem . . . . . . (venit, veniunt)
6 nūntius in forō . . . . . . (clāmat, clāmant)
7 senēs in forō . . . . . . (dormit, dormiunt)
8 pater . . . . . in tablīnō. (est, sunt)

3 Translate into English:

hodiē Pompēiānī sunt ōtiōsī. dominī et servī nōn labōrant. multī Pompēiānī in theātrō sedent. spectātōrēs Actium exspectant. tandem Actius in scaenā stat. Pompēiānī plaudunt.

subitō Pompēiānī magnum clāmōrem audiunt. servus theātrum intrat. "euge! fūnambulus adest," clāmat servus. 5 Pompēiānī Actium nōn spectant. omnēs Pompēiānī ē theātrō currunt et fūnambulum spectant.

nēmō in theātrō manet. Actius tamen nōn est īrātus. Actius quoque fūnambulum spectat.

multī	*many*
spectātōrēs	*spectators*
tandem	*at last*
in scaenā	*on stage*
plaudunt	*applaud, clap*
subitō	*suddenly*
fūnambulus	*tightrope walker*
nēmō	*no one*

About the Language

1 Study the following examples of singular and plural forms:

SINGULAR	PLURAL
servus ambulat.	**servī** ambulant.
The slave walks.	*The slaves walk.*
puella rīdet.	**puellae** rīdent.
The girl smiles.	*The girls smile.*
mercātor contendit.	**mercātōrēs** contendunt.
The merchant hurries.	*The merchants hurry.*

2 Each of the words in boldface is in the *nominative* case, because it refers to a person or people who are performing some action, such as walking or smiling.

3 **servus**, **puella**, and **mercātor** are therefore *nominative singular* and **servī**, **puellae**, and **mercātōrēs** are *nominative plural*.

The Theater at Pompeii

Plays were not performed in Pompeii every day, but only at festivals, which were held several times a year. When the notices appeared announcing a performance, there was great excitement in the town. On the day itself the stores were closed and no business was done in the forum. People set off for the theater early in the morning. Men, women, and slaves flocked through the streets, some carrying cushions, because the seats were made of stone, many taking food and drink for the day. The only people who did not need to hurry were the town officials and other important citizens, for whom the best seats at the front of the auditorium were reserved. These important people carried tickets which indicated the entrance they should use and where they were to sit. The tickets were made of bone or ivory and were often decorated with

engravings of the theater, actors' masks, fruit, or animals. Latecomers among the ordinary citizens had to be content with a seat right at the top of the large semicircular auditorium. The large theater at Pompeii could hold 5,000 people.

A dramatic performance was a public occasion, and admission to the theater was free. All the expenses were paid by a wealthy citizen, who provided the actors, the producer, the scenery, and costumes. He volunteered to do this, not only to benefit his fellow citizens, but also to gain popularity which would be useful in local political elections.

The performance consisted of a series of plays and lasted all day, even during the heat of the afternoon. To keep the spectators cool, a large canvas awning was suspended by ropes and pulleys across most of the theater. The awning was managed by sailors, who were used to handling ropes and canvas; even so, on a windy day the awning could not be unfurled, and the audience had to make use of hats or sunshades to protect themselves from the sun. Between plays, scented water was sprinkled by attendants.

One of the most popular kinds of production was the "pantomime," a mixture of opera and ballet. The plot, which was usually serious, was taken from the Greek myths. The parts of the different characters were mimed and danced by one masked performer, while a chorus sang the lyrics. An orchestra containing such instruments as the lyre, double pipes, trumpet, and castanets accompanied the performance, providing a rhythmical beat. Pantomime actors were usually Greek slaves or freedmen. They were much admired for their skill and stamina, and attracted a large following of fans.

Scene from a comedy. A young man returning drunk from a party is met by his angry father

Actor playing the part of a slave sitting on an altar

Equally popular were the comic actors, who played in vulgar farces about everyday life. The bronze statue of a comic actor, Sorex, was discovered in Pompeii, together with scribblings on walls naming other popular actors. One of these reads:

"Actius, our favorite, come back quickly."

Comic actors also appeared in the short one-act plays which were often put on at the end of longer performances. These short plays were about Italian country life and were packed with dirty jokes and horseplay. They used just a few familiar characters, such as Pappus, an old fool, and Manducus, a greedy clown. These characters were instantly recognizable from the strange masks worn by the actors. The Roman poet, Juvenal, describes a performance of a play of this kind in a country theater, where the children sitting on their mothers' laps shrank back in horror when they saw the gaping, white masks. These masks, like those used in other plays, were probably made of linen which was covered with plaster and painted.

Sometimes, at a festival, the old comedies of Plautus and Terence were put on. These plays also used a number of familiar characters, but the plots were complicated and the dialogue more witty than that of the farces. There is usually a young man from a respectable family who is leading a wild and carefree life; he is often in debt and in love with a

The large theater in Pompeii

pretty but unsuitable slave-girl. His father, who is old-fashioned and disapproving, has to be kept in the dark by deception. The son is usually helped in this by a smart slave, who gets himself and his young master in and out of trouble at great speed.

For example, in Plautus' play called the *Mostellaria (The Haunted House)*, a young man called Philolaches is having a very good time while his father is abroad. Philolaches has also borrowed a lot of money to buy the freedom of the slave-girl he loves. One day he is having a party with friends outside his house, when his slave Tranio interrupts the merrymaking to announce that Philolaches' father has returned unexpectedly and will arrive from the harbor at any moment. Amid the general panic, Tranio has an idea. He hustles Philolaches and his friends into the house and locks the door. The father now arrives. Tranio greets him respectfully but pretends that it is dangerous for him to go into the house because it is haunted.

Unfortunately, at this moment a moneylender turns up to claim the money borrowed by Philolaches. Tranio thinks quickly and pretends that the money was borrowed to buy the house next door. Even when Philolaches' father meets the real owner of the house, Tranio manages to hide the truth for some time, but he is found out at last and jumps onto the top of an altar to escape punishment. All ends happily, however, when one of Philolaches' friends arrives and persuades the father to forgive his son. Even Tranio is forgiven.

Words and Phrases Checklist

adest	*is here*	meus	*my, mine*
adsunt	*are here*	multus	*much*
agricola	*farmer*	multī	*many*
ambulat	*walks*	optimus	*very good, excellent, best*
audit	*hears, listens to*	petit	*heads for, attacks, seeks*
clāmor	*shout, uproar*	plaudit	*applauds, claps*
contendit	*hurries*	puella	*girl*
currit	*runs*	senex	*old man*
euge!	*hurrah!*	spectat	*looks at, watches*
fābula	*play, story*	stat	*stands*
fābulam agit	*acts in a play*	turba	*crowd*
fēmina	*woman*	ubi?	*where?*
hodiē	*today*	urbs	*city*
iuvenis	*young man*	venit	*comes*

Word Search

Match each definition with one of the words given below.

audience, convene, fabulous, feminine, spectator, state, turbulent

1 . . . . . : a group of listeners
2 . . . . . : mythical or legendary; marvelous
3 . . . . . : a condition or situation
4 . . . . . : to assemble, gather together
5 . . . . . : a person who watches
6 . . . . . : rowdy, unruly
7 . . . . . : characteristic of women

'Beware of the dog' – mosaic in entryway to house in Pompeii

Fēlīx

servī per viam ambulābant.

canis subitō lātrāvit.

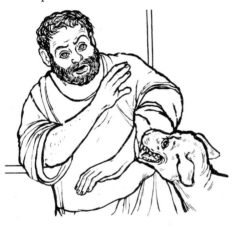

Grumiō canem timēbat.

"pestis!" clāmāvit coquus.

Clēmēns erat fortis.

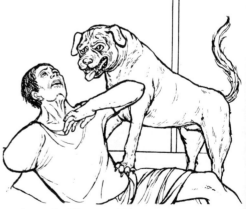

sed canis Clēmentem superāvit.

Quīntus per viam ambulābat.

iuvenis clāmōrem audīvit.

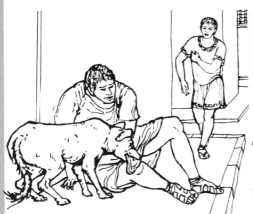

canis Clēmentem vexābat.

Quīntus canem pulsāvit.

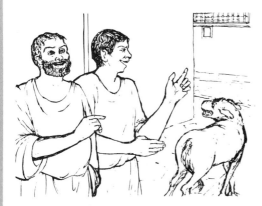

servī erant laetī.

servī Quīntum laudāvērunt.

pugna

Clēmēns in forō ambulābat. turba maxima erat in forō. servī et ancillae cibum emēbant. multī pistōrēs pānem vēndēbant. poēta recitābat. mercātor Graecus contentiōnem cum agricolā habēbat. mercātor īrātus pecūniam postulābat. subitō agricola Graecum pulsāvit, quod Graecus agricolam vituperābat. Pompēiānī 5 rīdēbant, et agricolam incitābant. Clēmēns, postquam clāmōrem audīvit, ad pugnam festīnāvit. tandem agricola mercātōrem superāvit et ē forō agitāvit. Pompēiānī agricolam fortem laudāvērunt.

Words and Phrases

pugna	*fight*	pulsāvit	*hit, punched*
maxima	*very large*	quod	*because*
erat	*was*	incitābant	*were urging on*
pistōrēs	*bakers*	postquam	*when, after*
pānem vēndēbant	*were selling bread*	festīnāvit	*hurried*
contentiōnem ... habēbat	*was having an argument*	superāvit	*overpowered*
cum agricolā	*with a farmer*	agitāvit	*chased*
postulābat	*was demanding*		

Fēlīx

multī Pompēiānī in tabernā vīnum bibēbant. Clēmēns tabernam intrāvit. subitō Clēmēns "Fēlīx!" clāmāvit. Clēmēns Fēlīcem laetē salūtāvit. Fēlīx erat lībertus.

Clēmēns Fēlīcem ad vīllam invītāvit. Clēmēns et Fēlīx vīllam intrāvērunt. Clēmēns Caecilium et Metellam quaesīvit. Caecilius in 5 tablīnō scrībēbat. Metella in hortō sedēbat. Caecilius et Metella ad ātrium festīnāvērunt et Fēlīcem salūtāvērunt. postquam Quīntus ātrium intrāvit, Fēlīx iuvenem spectāvit. lībertus erat valdē commōtus. paene lacrimābat; sed rīdēbat.

tum Clēmēns ad culīnam festīnāvit. Grumiō in culīnā dormiēbat. 10 Clēmēns coquum excitāvit et tōtam rem nārrāvit. coquus, quod erat laetus, cēnam optimam parāvit.

Atrium of the House of Menander

Words and Phrases

laetē	*happily*
lībertus	*freedman*
invītāvit	*invited*
valdē commōtus	*very moved, very much affected*
paene lacrimābat	*was almost weeping*
tum	*then*
excitāvit	*woke up, aroused*
tōtam rem	*the whole story*
nārrāvit	*told*
parāvit	*prepared*

Fēlīx et fūr

post cēnam Quīntus rogāvit, "pater, cūr Fēlīx nunc est lībertus? ōlim erat servus tuus."

   tum pater tōtam rem nārrāvit.

Caecilius: Fēlīx ōlim in tablīnō scrībēbat. Fēlīx erat sōlus. Clēmēns et Grumiō cibum in forō quaerēbant. Metella   5
aberat, quod sorōrem vīsitābat.

Fēlīx: pater tuus aberat, quod argentāriam in forō administrābat.

Caecilius: nēmō erat in vīllā nisi Fēlīx et īnfāns. parvus īnfāns in cubiculō dormiēbat. subitō fūr per iānuam intrāvit. fūr   10
tacitē ātrium circumspectāvit; tacitē cubiculum intrāvit, ubi īnfāns erat. Fēlīx nihil audīvit, quod intentē labōrābat. fūr parvum īnfantem ē vīllā tacitē portābat. subitō īnfāns vāgīvit. Fēlīx, postquam clāmōrem audīvit, statim ē tablīnō festīnāvit.   15

   "furcifer!" clāmāvit Fēlīx īrātus, et fūrem ferōciter pulsāvit. Fēlīx fūrem paene necāvit. ita Fēlīx parvum īnfantem servāvit.

Fēlīx: dominus, postquam rem audīvit, erat laetus et mē līberāvit. ego igitur sum lībertus.   20

Quīntus: sed quis erat īnfāns?

Caecilius: erat Quīntus!

Words and Phrases

fūr	*thief*	in cubiculō	*in a bedroom*
post	*after*	tacitē	*quietly, silently*
rogāvit	*asked*	ubi	*where*
nunc	*now*	nihil	*nothing*
ōlim	*once, some time ago*	portābat	*began to carry*
sōlus	*alone*	vāgīvit	*cried, wailed*
aberat	*was out*	statim	*at once*
sorōrem	*sister*	necāvit	*killed*
administrābat	*was managing*	ita	*in this way*
nisi	*except*	servāvit	*saved*
īnfāns	*baby, child*	līberāvit	*freed, set free*
parvus	*small*	igitur	*therefore, and so*

About the Language

1 The sentences in the first five Stages have all been in the *present tense*. Study the following examples:

PRESENT TENSE

SINGULAR	servus **labōrat.**	*The slave works.*
PLURAL	servī **labōrant.**	*The slaves work.*

2 In Stage 6, you have met the *imperfect tense* and the *perfect tense*. Study the different endings of the two tenses and their English translation:

IMPERFECT TENSE

SINGULAR	poēta **recitābat.**	*A poet was reciting.*
	Metella in hortō **sedēbat.**	*Metella was sitting in the garden.*
PLURAL	Pompēiānī vīnum **bibēbant.**	*The Pompeians were drinking wine.*
	servī in forō **ambulābant.**	*The slaves were walking in the forum.*

PERFECT TENSE

SINGULAR	Clēmēns clāmōrem **audīvit.**	*Clemens heard the uproar.*
	coquus **intrāvit.**	*The cook entered.*
PLURAL	amīcī Caecilium **salūtāvērunt.**	*The friends greeted Caecilius.*
	iuvenēs ad tabernam **festīnāvērunt.**	*The young men hurried to an inn.*

3 Compare the endings of the imperfect and perfect tenses with the present tense. Notice that in all three tenses the singular ends in **-t** and the plural in **-nt.**

4 Notice how Latin shows the difference between *is, are* and *was, were*:

PRESENT	IMPERFECT
Caecilius **est** in tablīnō.	Caecilius **erat** in forō.
Caecilius is in the study.	*Caecilius was in the forum.*
servī **sunt** in culīnā.	servī **erant** in viā.
The slaves are in the kitchen.	*The slaves were in the street.*

Practicing the Language

1 Read the following story, and then answer the questions at the end.
Write your answers in English.

avārus

duo fūrēs ōlim ad vīllam contendēbant. in vīllā mercātor habitābat.
mercātor erat senex et avārus. avārus multam pecūniam habēbat.
fūrēs, postquam vīllam intrāvērunt, ātrium circumspectāvērunt.

"avārus," inquit fūr, "est sōlus. avārus servum nōn habet."

tum fūrēs tablīnum intrāvērunt. avārus clāmāvit et ferōciter   5
pugnāvit, sed fūrēs senem facile superāvērunt.

"ubi est pecūnia, senex?" rogāvit fūr.

"servus fidēlis pecūniam in cubiculō custōdit," inquit senex.

"tū servum fidēlem nōn habēs, quod avārus es," clāmāvit fūr.
tum fūrēs cubiculum petīvērunt.   10

"pecūniam videō," inquit fūr. fūrēs cubiculum intrāvērunt, ubi
pecūnia erat, et pecūniam intentē spectāvērunt. sed ēheu! ingēns
serpēns in pecūniā iacēbat. fūrēs serpentem timēbant et ē vīllā
celeriter festīnāvērunt.

in vīllā avārus rīdēbat et serpentem laudābat.   15

"tū es optimus servus. numquam dormīs. pecūniam meam
semper servās."

Words and Phrases

avārus	*miser*
duo	*two*
habitābat	*was living*
inquit	*said*
pugnāvit	*fought*
facile	*easily*
fidēlis	*faithful*
custōdit	*is guarding*
ingēns	*huge*
serpēns	*snake*
iacēbat	*was lying*
timēbant	*were afraid of, feared*
celeriter	*quickly*
numquam	*never*
servās	*protect*

Questions

1 How many thieves were there?
2 What did the thieves do immediately after they had entered the house?
3 Why did one of the thieves think the miser would be alone?
4 Who won the fight and why?
5 Where was the money?
6 Why did the thieves run away?
7 What did the miser think of the snake and why?

Lararium of the House of the Vettii

2 Complete each sentence with the right word. Write out the completed sentence in Latin and then translate it.

for example: . . . . . in forō ambulābat. (servus, servī)
servus in forō ambulābat.
The slave was walking in the forum.

. . . . . forum spectābant. (amīcus, amīcī)
amīcī forum spectābant.
The friends were looking at the forum.

1 . . . . . per viam festīnābat. (lībertus, lībertī)
2 . . . . . pecūniam portābant. (servus, servī)
3 . . . . . ātrium circumspectāvit. (fūr, fūrēs)
4 . . . . . clāmōrem audīvērunt. (mercātor, mercātōrēs)
5 . . . . . fūrem superāvērunt. (puer, puerī)
6 . . . . . ad urbem festīnāvit. (nauta, nautae)

Slaves and Freedmen

Wherever you traveled in the Roman world, you would find people who were slaves, like Grumio, Clemens, and Melissa. They belonged to a master or mistress, to whom they had to give complete obedience; they were not free to make decisions for themselves; they could not marry; nor could they own personal possessions or be protected by the law. The law, in fact, did not regard them as human beings, but as things that could be bought and sold, treated well or treated badly. These people carried out much of the hard manual work but they also took part in many skilled trades and occupations. They did not live separately from free people; many slaves would live in the same house as their master and occupy rooms in the rear part of the house. Slaves and free people could often be found working together.

The Romans and others who lived around the Mediterranean in Classical times regarded slavery as a normal and necessary part of life; even those who realized that it was not a natural thing made no serious effort to abolish it. Good masters showed kindness to their slaves by giving them decent living conditions, by taking care of them, and sometimes by setting them free.

People usually became slaves as a result either of being taken prisoner during a time of war or of being captured by pirates; the children of slaves were born into slavery. They came from many different tribes and countries, Gaul and Britain, Spain and North Africa, Egypt, different parts of Greece and Asia Minor, Syria and Palestine. By the time of the Emperor Augustus at the beginning of the first century A.D., there were perhaps as many as three slaves for every five free citizens in Italy. Most families owned at least one or two; a merchant like Caecilius would have no fewer than a dozen in his house and many more working on his estates and in his businesses. Very wealthy men owned hundreds and sometimes even thousands of slaves. A man called Pedanius Secundus, who lived in Rome, kept four hundred in his house there; when one of them murdered him, they were all put to death, in spite of protests by the people of Rome.

Slaves were employed in all kinds of work. In the country, their life was rougher and harsher than in the cities. They worked on farms, on big cattle ranches in southern Italy, in the mines, and on the building of roads and bridges. Some of the strongest slaves were bought for training as gladiators.

Two customers (sitting down), attended by a slave, are inspecting a piece of cloth. The salesman in the center and his assistants may also be slaves.

In the towns, slaves were used for both unskilled and skilled work. They were cooks and gardeners, general servants, laborers in factories, secretaries, musicians, actors, and entertainers. In the course of doing such jobs, they were regularly in touch with their masters and other free men; they moved freely about the streets of the towns, went shopping, visited temples, and were also quite often present in the theater and at shows in the amphitheater. Foreign visitors to Rome and Italy were sometimes rather surprised that there was so little visible difference between a slave and a poor free man.

Some masters were cruel and brutal to their slaves, but others were kind and humane. Common sense usually prevented a master from treating his slaves too harshly, since only healthy, well-cared-for slaves were likely to work efficiently. A slave who was a skilled craftsman, particularly one who was able to read and write, keep accounts, and manage the work of a small store, would have cost a large sum of money, and a Roman master was generally too prudent to waste an expensive possession through carelessness.

Not every slave remained in slavery until the end of his life. Freedom was sometimes given as a reward for particularly good service, sometimes as a sign of friendship and respect. Freedom was also very commonly given at the death of a master by a statement in his will. But the law laid down certain limits. For example, a slave could not be freed before he was thirty years old.

The act of freeing a slave was called **manūmissiō**. This word is connected with two other words, **manus** (*hand*) and **mittō** (*send*), and means *a sending out from the hand* or *setting free from control*. Manumission was performed in several ways. One method, the oldest, took the form of a legal ceremony before a public official, such as a judge. A witness claimed that the slave did not really belong to the master at all; the master did not deny the claim; the slave's head was then touched with a rod, and he was declared officially free. There were other simpler methods. A master might manumit his slave by declaring him free in the presence of friends at home or merely by inviting him to recline on the couch at dinner.

The ex-slave became a **lībertus** (*freedman*). He now had the opportunity to make his own way in life, and possibly to become an important member of his community. He did not, however, receive all the privileges of a citizen who had been born free. He could not stand as a candidate in public elections, nor could he become a high-ranking officer in the army. It was common for a freedman to become one of the clientes

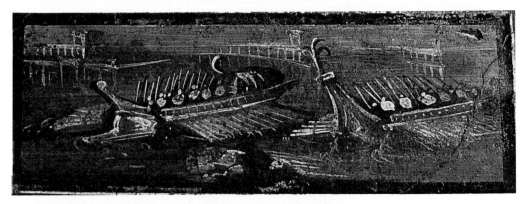

Wall-painting from the House of the Vettii: warships

of his former master; he would visit him regularly to pay his respects, usually at the start of the morning, and help and support him whenever he could. This connection between them is seen very clearly in the names taken by a freedman. Suppose that his slave-name had been Felix and his master had been Lucius Caecilius Iucundus. As soon as he became free, Felix would take some of the names of his former master and call himself Lucius Caecilius Felix.

Some freedmen continued to do the same work that they had previously done as slaves; others were set up in business by their former masters. Others became priests in the temples or servants of the town governing board; the board secretaries, messengers, town clerk, and town crier were all probably freedmen. Some became very rich and powerful. Two freedmen at Pompeii, who were called the Vettii and were possibly brothers, owned a house which is one of the most magnificent in the town. The colorful paintings on its walls and the elegant marble fountains in the garden show clearly how prosperous the Vettii were. Another Pompeian freedman was the architect who designed the large theater; another was the father of Lucius Caecilius Iucundus.

Words and Phrases Checklist

abest   *is out, is absent*
  aberat   *was out, was absent*
avārus   *miser*
cubiculum   *bedroom*
emit   *buys*
erat   *was*
ferōciter   *fiercely*
festīnat   *hurries*
fortis   *brave* (also *strong* in other contexts)
fūr   *thief*
īnfāns   *baby, child*
intentē   *intently*
lībertus   *freedman, ex-slave*
ōlim   *once, some time ago*
parvus   *small*
per   *through*
postquam   *after, when*
pulsat   *hits, punches, whacks*
quod   *because*
rēs   *thing*
scrībit   *writes*
subitō   *suddenly*
superat   *overcomes, overpowers*
tum   *then*
tuus   *your, yours*
vituperat   *finds fault with, tells off, curses*

Word Search

Match each definition with one of the words given below.

avarice, cubicle, ferocity, infant, inscribe, insuperable, pulse

1 . . . . . : fierceness
2 . . . . . : to write on or engrave
3 . . . . . : greed
4 . . . . . : a beat or rhythm
5 . . . . . : a small room
6 . . . . . : a baby
7 . . . . . : invincible, unbeatable

cēna

amīcus Caecilium vīsitābat.
vīllam intrāvit.

Caecilius amīcum exspectābat.
amīcum salūtāvit.

amīcus cum Caeciliō cēnābat.
cēnam laudāvit.

amīcus pōculum īnspexit.
vīnum gustāvit.

amīcus pōculum hausit.
tum fābulam nārrāvit.

Caecilius plausit.
"euge!" dīxit.

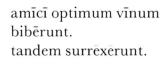

amīcī optimum vīnum
bibērunt.
tandem surrexērunt.

servī in ātriō stābant.
iānuam aperuērunt.

Caecilius et amīcus "valē"
dīxērunt.
amīcus ē vīllā discessit.

fābula mīrābilis

multī amīcī cum Caeciliō cēnābant. Fēlīx quoque aderat. omnēs amīcī coquum laudāvērunt, quod cēna erat optima.

postquam omnēs cēnāvērunt, Caecilius clāmāvit, "ubi est Decēns? Decēns nōn adest." tum Caecilius Clēmentem ē vīllā mīsit. servus Decentem per urbem quaesīvit. 5

postquam servus ē vīllā discessit, Fēlīx pōculum hausit. tum lībertus fābulam mīrābilem nārrāvit:

"ōlim amīcus meus ex urbe discēdēbat. nox erat lūcida, quod lūna plēna lūcēbat. amīcus per viam festīnābat, ubi silva erat, et subitō centuriōnem cōnspexit. amīcus meus centuriōnem salūtāvit. 10 centuriō tamen nihil dīxit. tum centuriō tunicam dēposuit. ecce! centuriō ēvānuit. ingēns lupus subitō appāruit. amīcus meus valdē timēbat. ingēns lupus ululāvit et ad silvam festīnāvit. tunica in viā iacēbat. amīcus tunicam cautē īnspexit. ecce! tunica erat lapidea. tum amīcus rem intellēxit. ille centuriō erat versipellis." 15

Words and Phrases

		cōnspexit	*caught sight of*
fābula	*story*	dīxit	*said*
mīrābilis	*marvelous, strange*	tunicam	*tunic*
mīsit	*sent*	dēposuit	*took off*
discessit	*departed, left*	ēvānuit	*vanished*
pōculum hausit	*drained his wine-cup*	lupus	*wolf*
ex urbe	*from the city*	appāruit	*appeared*
nox	*night*	ululāvit	*howled*
lūcida	*bright*	cautē	*cautiously*
lūna	*moon*	īnspexit	*looked at, examined*
plēna	*full*	lapidea	*made of stone*
lūcēbat	*was shining*	rem intellēxit	*understood the truth*
silva	*woods, forest*	ille centuriō	*that centurion*
centuriōnem	*centurion*	versipellis	*werewolf*

About the Language

1 Study the following example:

mercātor Caecilium vīsitābat. mercator vīllam intrāvit.
A merchant was visiting Caecilius.   The merchant entered the house.

2 In Stage 7, you have met a shorter way of saying this:

mercātor Caecilium vīsitābat. vīllam intrāvit.
A merchant was visiting Caecilius. He entered the house.

The following sentences behave in the same way:

amīcī cum Caeciliō cēnābant. coquum laudāvērunt.
Some friends were dining with Caecilius. They praised the cook.

ancilla in ātriō stābat. dominum salūtāvit.
The slave-girl was standing in the atrium. She greeted the master.

3 Further examples for study and translation:

1 Grumiō in culīnā labōrābat. cēnam parābat.
2 āctōrēs in theātrō clāmābant. fābulam agēbant.
3 Metella nōn erat in vīllā. in hortō ambulābat.
4 lībertī in tabernā bibēbant. Grumiōnem salūtāvērunt.
5 iuvenis pōculum hausit. vīnum laudāvit.

4 Notice that Latin does not usually include a separate word for *he*, *she*, or *they*.

Decēns

postquam Fēlīx fābulam nārrāvit, omnēs plausērunt. tum omnēs tacēbant et
aliam fābulam exspectābant. subitō Caecilius et hospitēs clāmōrem audīvērunt.
omnēs ad ātrium festīnāvērunt, ubi Clēmēns stābat.

Caecilius:	hercle! quid est? cūr tū clāmōrem facis?
Clēmēns:	Decēns, Decēns . . .
Caecilius:	quid est?
Clēmēns:	Decēns est mortuus.
omnēs:	quid? mortuus? ēheu!

(duo servī intrant.)

Caecilius: quid dīcis? 10

servus prīmus: dominus meus ad vīllam tuam veniēbat; dominus gladiātōrem prope amphitheātrum cōnspexit.

servus secundus: gladiātor dominum terruit, quod gladium ingentem vibrābat. tum gladiātor clāmāvit,

"tū mē nōn terrēs, leō, tū mē nōn terrēs! leōnēs 15 amīcum meum in arēnā necāvērunt, sed tū mē nōn terrēs!"

Decēns valdē timēbat.

"tū es īnsānus," inquit dominus. "ego nōn sum leō. sum homō." 20

gladiātor tamen dominum ferōciter petīvit et eum ad amphitheātrum trāxit. dominus perterritus clāmāvit. Clēmēns clāmōrem audīvit. Clēmēns, quod fortis erat, amphitheātrum intrāvit. Decentem in arēnā cōnspexit. dominus 25 meus erat mortuus.

Caecilius: ego rem intellegō! gladiātor erat Pugnāx. Pugnāx erat gladiātor nōtissimus. Pugnāx ōlim in arēnā pugnābat, et leō Pugnācem necāvit. Pugnāx nōn vīvit: Pugnāx est umbra. umbra Decentem 30 necāvit.

Words and Phrases

plausērunt	*applauded*
tacēbant	*were silent*
aliam	*another*
hospitēs	*guests*
hercle!	*by Hercules!*
mortuus	*dead*
prīmus	*first*
gladiātōrem	*gladiator*
prope amphitheātrum	*near the amphitheater*
secundus	*second*
terruit	*frightened*
gladium	*sword*
ingentem	*huge*
vibrābat	*was brandishing, was waving*
in arēnā	*in the arena*
īnsānus	*insane, crazy*
homō	*man*
eum	*him*
trāxit	*dragged*
nōtissimus	*very well-known*
vīvit	*is alive*
umbra	*ghost*

The amphitheater in Pompeii

post cēnam

postquam Caecilius rem explicāvit, omnēs amīcī tacēbant. mox amīcī "valē" dīxērunt et ē vīllā discessērunt. per viam timidē prōcēdēbant. nūllae stēllae lūcēbant. nūlla lūna erat in caelō. amīcī nihil audīvērunt, quod viae dēsertae erant. amīcī per urbem tacitē prōcēdēbant, quod umbram timēbant.   5

    subitō fēlēs ululāvit. amīcī valdē timēbant. omnēs per urbem perterritī ruērunt, quod dē vītā dēspērābant. clāmōrem mīrābilem faciēbant. multī Pompēiānī erant sollicitī, quod clāmōrem audīvērunt. Caecilius tamen clāmōrēm nōn audīvit, quod in cubiculō dormiēbat.   10

Words and Phrases

explicāvit	*explained*
valē	*good-by*
timidē	*fearfully*
prōcēdēbant	*were advancing, were proceeding*
nūllae stēllae	*no stars*
in caelō	*in the sky*
dēsertae	*deserted*
fēlēs	*cat*
ruērunt	*rushed*
dē vītā dēspērābant	*were despairing for their life*
sollicitī	*worried, anxious*

About the Language

1 In Stage 6 you met examples of the perfect tense. They looked like this:

> senex ad tabernam **ambulāvit.**
> *The old man walked to the inn.*

> amīcī in urbe **dormīvērunt.**
> *The friends slept in the city.*

This is the commonest way in which Latin forms the perfect tense.

2 In Stage 7 you have met other common forms of the perfect tense. Compare them with their imperfect forms:

	IMPERFECT	PERFECT
SINGULAR	appārēbat	appāruit
	he was appearing	*he appeared*
	dīcēbat	dīxit
	he was saying	*he said*
	discēdēbat	discessit
	he was departing	*he departed*
PLURAL	appārēbant	appāruērunt
	they were appearing	*they appeared*
	dīcēbant	dīxērunt
	they were saying	*they said*
	discēdēbant	discessērunt
	they were departing	*they departed*

3 If you are not sure whether a particular word is in the present tense or the perfect tense, you can check by looking it up in the "Complete Vocabulary" section, beginning on page 213.

Practicing the Language

1 Complete each sentence with the right phrase, and then translate it.

for example: amīcī . . . . . . (vīllam intrāvit, cēnam laudāvērunt)
amīcī cēnam laudāvērunt.
The friends praised the dinner.

1 mercātor . . . . . . (ē vīllā discessit, clāmōrem audīvērunt)
2 amīcī . . . . . . (pōculum īnspexit, rem intellēxērunt)
3 leōnēs . . . . . . (gladiātōrem terruit, gladiātōrem cōnspexērunt)
4 lībertī . . . . . . (lūnam spectāvit, ad portum festīnāvērunt)
5 centuriō . . . . . . (fābulam audīvit, servum laudāvērunt)
6 fūr . . . . . . (per urbem ruit, centuriōnem terruērunt)
7 Caecilius et amīcus . . . . . . (leōnem cōnspexit, portum petīvērunt)
8 ancillae . . . . . . (ad vīllam ambulāvit, in vīllā dormīvērunt)

2 Complete each sentence with the right word, and then translate it.

for example: . . . . . cēnam parāvit. (coquus, coquum)
     coquus cēnam parāvit.
     The cook prepared the dinner.

 1 Clēmēns . . . . . excitāvit. (coquus, coquum)
 2 . . . . . fābulam nārrāvit. (lībertus, lībertum)
 3 . . . . . gladiātōrem cōnspexērunt. (amīcus, amīcī)
 4 . . . . . ad forum festīnāvērunt. (agricola, agricolae)
 5 ancilla . . . . . aperuit. (iānua, iānuam)
 6 . . . . . clāmōrem audīvit. (poēta, poētae)
 7 fūrēs . . . . . necāvērunt. (centuriō, centuriōnem)
 8 . . . . . cēnam laudāvit. (gladiātor, gladiātōrem)
 9 . . . . . cibum ad theātrum portāvērunt. (spectātor, spectātōrēs)
 10 . . . . . ē vīllā discessit. (senex, senēs)

Relief showing a boar hunt

vēnātiō

Quīntus amīcum suum vīsitābat. amīcus erat Gāius. Gāius erat vir fortis et vēnātor. in vīllā magnificā habitābat. Quīntus, postquam ad hanc vīllam vēnit, ātrium intrāvit. pictūra pretiōsa et maxima erat in ātriō. vēnātōrēs et canēs et cervī erant in pictūrā. Gāius hanc pictūram amābat, quod pulcherrima erat. 5

postquam Quīntus amīcum salūtāvit, Gāius dīxit:

"tū opportūnē venīs. ingēns aper latet in monte Vesuviō. servī meī sunt ignāvī; aprum timent. num tū timēs?"

"aper est animal ferōx," respondit iuvenis. "ego tamen nōn timeō." 10

tum Quīntus longum vēnābulum cēpit et amīcī ad vēnātiōnem contendērunt. multī servī et multī canēs aderant. omnēs ad montem prōcessērunt, ubi aper latēbat.

servī, postquam aprum vīdērunt, clāmōrem fēcērunt. aper ferōx, quod clāmōrem audīvit, impetum fēcit. Quīntus fortiter prōcessit et 15 vēnābulum ēmīsit. ecce! aprum trānsfīxit. ingēns aper ad terram mortuus dēcidit. multus sanguis ex ōre fluēbat.

Words and Phrases

vēnātiō	*hunt*	animal	*animal*
suum	*his*	ferōx	*ferocious*
vir	*man*	longum	*long*
vēnātor	*hunter*	vēnābulum	*hunting spear*
magnificā	*magnificent*	cēpit	*took*
hanc	*this*	prōcessērunt	*proceeded, advanced*
vēnit	*came*	vīdērunt	*saw*
pretiōsa	*precious, expensive*	clāmōrem ⎫	⎰ *made a noise,*
cervī	*deer*	fēcērunt ⎭	⎱ *shouted*
amābat	*liked, loved*	impetum fēcit	*made an attack, charged*
pulcherrima	*very beautiful*	fortiter	*bravely*
opportūnē	*just at the right time*	vēnābulum ēmīsit	*threw his spear*
aper	*boar*	trānsfīxit	*pierced*
latet	*lies hidden*	terram	*ground*
ignāvī	*cowards*	dēcidit	*fell down*
num tū ⎫	⎰ *surely* you *are*	ex ōre	*from its mouth*
timēs? ⎭	⎱ *not afraid?*		

Names and Proper Adjectives

in monte Vesuviō   *on Mount Vesuvius*

Metella et Melissa

Metella Melissam in vīllā quaerēbat. Metella culīnam intrāvit, ubi
Grumiō labōrābat. Grumiō erat īrātus.

"cūr tū es īrātus, Grumiō? cūr ferōciter circumspectās?" rogāvit
Metella.

"heri Melissa cēnam optimam parāvit," respondit coquus.   5
"hodiē ego cēnam pessimam parō, quod nūllus cibus adest. heri
multus cibus erat in culīnā. ancilla omnem cibum coxit."

Metella ē culīnā discessit et ad tablīnum festīnāvit, ubi Clēmēns
labōrābat. Clēmēns quoque erat īrātus.

"Melissa est pestis!" clāmāvit servus.   10

"quid fēcit Melissa?" rogāvit Metella.

"heri Melissa in tablīnō labōrābat," respondit Clēmēns. "hodiē
ego in tablīnō labōrō. ecce! cērae et stilī absunt. nihil est in locō
propriō."

Metella, postquam ē tablīnō discessit, hortum intrāvit. Metella   15
Melissam in hortō vīdit. ēheu! ancilla lacrimābat.

"Melissa, cūr lacrimās?" rogāvit Metella.

"lacrimō quod Grumiō et Clēmēns mē vituperant," respondit
ancilla.

"ego tamen tē nōn vituperō," inquit Metella. "ego tē laudō. ecce!   20
tū crīnēs meōs optimē compōnis. stolam meam optimē compōnis.
fortasse Grumiō et Clēmēns tē nōn laudant; sed ego tē laudō, quod
mē dīligenter cūrās."

Words and Phrases

heri	*yesterday*
pessimam	*very bad*
coxit	*cooked*
stilī	*pens (used for writing on wax tablets)*
in locō propriō	*in the right place*
crīnēs	*hair*
optimē	*very well*
compōnis	*arrange*
stolam	*(long) dress*
fortasse	*perhaps*
dīligenter	*carefully*
cūrās	*take care of*

About the Language

1 Notice how the following words form their perfect tense. Compare their present and perfect forms.

PRESENT		PERFECT	
facit	faciunt	fēcit	fēcērunt
he makes	*they make*	*he made*	*they made*
capit	capiunt	cēpit	cēpērunt
he takes	*they take*	*he took*	*they took*

2 Compare this with the way some words behave in English:

I run	I ran
I give	I gave
I come	I came

Roman Beliefs about Life after Death

The Romans did not place the tombs of the dead in a quiet, lonely place, but by the side of the road just outside the town, where they could be seen and admired by the passers-by. The tombs at Pompeii can still be seen along the roads that go north from the Herculaneum Gate and south from the Nuceria Gate.

Some were grand and impressive and looked like small houses; others were much more plain and simple. It was a common custom to decorate them with garlands of flowers and put offerings of food and wine before them.

In burying the dead along busy roads, and not in a peaceful cemetery, the Romans were not showing any lack of respect. On the contrary, they believed that unless the dead were properly buried and looked after, their ghosts would haunt the living and possibly do them harm. It was most important to provide a dead person with a tomb or grave, where the ghost could have a home. But it was also thought that he or she would want to be close to the life of the living. One tomb has this inscription: "I see and I gaze upon all who come from and to the city," and another,

Tombs outside the Nuceria Gate

"Lollius has been placed by the side of the road in order that all passers-by may say to him, 'Good morning, Lollius.'"

It was believed that the dead in some way continued the activities of life, and therefore had to be supplied with the things they would need. A hunter would want his spear, a farmer his farming tools, a woman her spindle. If the body of the dead person was buried, certain possessions were buried with the corpse; if it was cremated, possessions were burned along with it.

A Greek writer called Lucian tells the story of a husband who had burned all his dead wife's jewelry and clothes on the funeral pyre, so that she might have them in the next world. A week later he was trying to comfort himself by reading a book about life after death, when the ghost of his wife appeared. She began to reproach him because he had not burned one of her gilded sandals, which, she said, was lying under a chest. The family dog then barked and the ghost disappeared. The husband looked under the chest, found the sandal, and burned it.

The ghosts of the dead were also thought to be hungry and thirsty, and therefore had to be given food and drink. Offerings of eggs, beans, lentils, flour, and wine were placed regularly at the tomb. Sometimes holes were made in the tomb so that wine could be poured inside. Wine was offered because it was a convenient substitute for blood, the favorite drink of the dead. However, at the funeral and on special occasions animals were sacrificed, and their blood offered.

It was thought, however, that in spite of these attempts to take care of them, the dead did not lead a very happy existence. So that they might forget their unhappiness, their tombs were often decorated with flowers and surrounded by little gardens, a custom which has lasted to this day, although its original meaning has changed. With the same purpose in mind, the family and friends of a dead man held a banquet after the funeral and on the anniversary of his death. Sometimes these banquets took place in a dining-room attached to the tomb itself, sometimes in the family home. The ghosts of the dead were thought to attend and enjoy these cheerful occasions.

Some people also believed in an underworld where the wicked were punished for the misdeeds they had committed when alive, and where the good lived happily forever. Stories were told about the punishments suffered by famous evildoers such as the wicked Tityus, who had his liver pecked out by vultures, and the daughters of Danaus, who were condemned to pour water forever into jars that had holes in the bottom. In the first century A.D. most people did not take these stories seriously, but they continued to tell them to disobedient children to make them behave themselves.

There were a few people who did not believe in any form of life after death. These were the followers of a Greek called Epicurus, who taught that, when a person died, the breath that gave him or her life dissolved into the air and was lost forever. Men and women, therefore, had no need to fear the next world, and could devote all their energies to making the most of this one.

Words and Phrases Checklist

cēnat	*eats dinner, dines*	omnis	*all*
centuriō	*centurion*	parat	*prepares*
cōnspicit	*catches sight of*	pestis	*pest, rascal*
cum	*with*	pōculum	*cup (often for wine)*
facit	*makes, does*	prōcēdit	*advances, proceeds*
heri	*yesterday*	prope	*near*
ingēns	*huge*	pulcher	*beautiful*
intellegit	*understands*	rogat	*asks*
lacrimat	*cries, weeps*	tacitē	*quietly, silently*
mortuus	*dead*	tamen	*however*
nārrat	*tells, relates*	terret	*frightens*
necat	*kills*	umbra	*ghost, shadow*
nihil	*nothing*	valdē	*very much, very*

Word Search

Match each definition with one of the words given below.

conspicuous, intelligible, interrogation, omnipotent, pestilence, procedure, tacit

1 . . . . . : silent; unspoken
2 . . . . . : easily noticed, obvious
3 . . . . . : the act of questioning
4 . . . . . : understandable
5 . . . . . : a method; a course of action
6 . . . . . : all-powerful
7 . . . . . : a plague

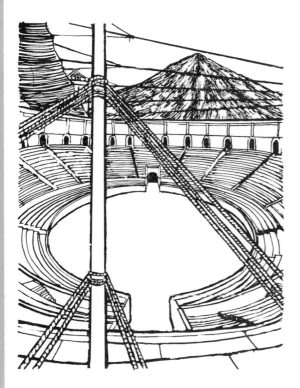

gladiātōrēs

nūntiī spectāculum nūntiābant.
Pompēiānī nūntiōs audiēbant.

gladiātōrēs per viam
prōcēdēbant.
Pompēiānī gladiātōrēs
laudābant.

puellae iuvenēs salūtāvērunt.
iuvenēs quoque ad
amphitheātrum contendēbant.

servī fēminās spectābant, quod
fēminae ad spectāculum
contendēbant.

puerī per viam festīnābant.
puellae puerōs salūtāvērunt.

Pompēiānī tabernās nōn
intrābant, quod tabernae
erant clausae.

Pompēiānī gladiātōrēs intentē
spectābant, quod gladiātōrēs
in arēnā pugnābant.

postquam gladiātōrēs
Pompēiānōs salūtāvērunt,
Pompēiānī plausērunt.

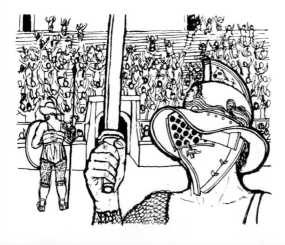

spectātōrēs murmillōnēs
incitābant, quod murmillōnēs
saepe victōrēs erant.

gladiātōrēs

Rēgulus erat senātor Rōmānus. in vīllā magnificā habitābat. vīlla erat prope Nūceriam. Nūcerīnī et Pompēiānī erant inimīcī. Nūcerīnī, quod amphitheātrum nōn habēbant, saepe ad amphitheātrum Pompēiānum veniēbant; saepe erant turbulentī.

Rēgulus ōlim spectāculum splendidum in amphitheātrō ēdidit,   5
quod diem nātālem celebrābat. multī Nūcerīnī igitur ad urbem vēnērunt. cīvēs Pompēiānī erant īrātī, quod Nūcerīnī viās complēbant. omnēs tamen ad forum contendērunt, ubi nūntiī erant. nūntiī spectāculum optimum nūntiābant:

"gladiātōrēs adsunt! vīgintī gladiātōrēs hodiē pugnant! rētiāriī   10
adsunt! murmillōnēs adsunt! bēstiāriī bēstiās ferōcēs agitant!"

Pompēiānī, postquam nūntiōs audīvērunt, ad amphitheātrum quam celerrimē contendērunt. Nūcerīnī quoque ad amphitheātrum festīnāvērunt. multī Pompēiānī igitur nōn intrāvērunt. hī Pompēiānī Nūcerīnōs et Rēgulum vituperābant, quod tōta cavea   15
plēna erat. spectātōrēs tamen prīmam pugnam exspectābant.

Words and Phrases

senātor	*senator*	cīvēs	*citizens*
inimīcī	*enemies*	complēbant	*were filling*
saepe	*often*	nūntiābant	*were announcing*
turbulentī	*rowdy, disorderly*	vīgintī	*twenty*
spectāculum	*show, spectacle*	bēstiāriī	*beast-fighters*
splendidum	*splendid*	bēstiās	*wild animals, beasts*
ēdidit	*presented*	quam celerrimē	*as quickly as possible*
diem nātālem	*birthday*	hī	*these*
celebrābat	*was celebrating*	cavea	*seating area*

Names and Proper Adjectives

Rōmānus	*Roman*
Nūceriam	*Nuceria*
Nūcerīnī	*Nucerians, citizens of Nuceria*

Wall-painting of gladiators

Gladiator's helmet and greaves

in arēnā

duo rētiāriī et duo murmillōnēs arēnam intrāvērunt. postquam gladiātōrēs spectātōrēs salūtāvērunt, tuba sonuit. tum gladiātōrēs pugnam commīsērunt. murmillōnēs Pompēiānōs valdē dēlectābant, quod saepe victōrēs erant. Pompēiānī igitur murmillōnēs incitābant. sed rētiāriī, quod erant expedītī, 5 murmillōnēs facile ēvītāvērunt.

"rētiāriī nōn pugnant! rētiāriī sunt ignāvī!" clāmāvērunt Pompēiānī. Nūcerīnī tamen respondērunt, "rētiāriī sunt callidī! rētiāriī murmillōnēs dēcipiunt!"

murmillōnēs rētiāriōs frūstrā ad pugnam prōvocāvērunt. tum 10 murmillō clāmāvit, "ūnus murmillō facile duōs rētiāriōs superat."

Pompēiānī plausērunt. tum murmillō rētiāriōs statim petīvit. murmillō et rētiāriī ferōciter pugnāvērunt. rētiāriī tandem murmillōnem graviter vulnerāvērunt. tum rētiāriī alterum murmillōnem petīvērunt. hic murmillō fortiter pugnāvit, sed 15 rētiāriī eum quoque superāvērunt.

Pompēiānī, quod īrātī erant, murmillōnēs vituperābant; missiōnem tamen postulābant, quod murmillōnēs fortēs erant. Nūcerīnī mortem postulābant. omnēs spectātōrēs tacēbant, et Rēgulum intentē spectābant. Rēgulus, quod Nūcerīnī mortem 20 postulābant, pollicem vertit. Pompēiānī erant īrātī, et vehementer clāmābant. rētiāriī tamen, postquam Rēgulus signum dedit, murmillōnēs interfēcērunt.

Words and Phrases

tuba	*trumpet*	graviter	*seriously*
sonuit	*sounded*	vulnerāvērunt	*wounded*
pugnam commīsērunt	*{began the fight*	alterum	*the second*
		hic	*this*
victōrēs	*victors, winners*	missiōnem	*release*
expedītī	*lightly armed*	mortem	*death*
ēvītāvērunt	*avoided*	pollicem vertit	*turned his thumb up*
callidī	*clever, smart*	vehementer	*violently, loudly*
dēcipiunt	*are deceiving, are tricking*	signum	*sign, signal*
frūstrā	*in vain*	dedit	*gave*
prōvocāvērunt	*challenged*	interfēcērunt	*killed*
ūnus	*one*		

About the Language

1 From Stage 2 onwards, you have met sentences like these:

amīcus **puellam** salūtat.   *The friend greets the girl.*
dominus **servum** vituperābat.   *The master was cursing the slave.*
nautae **mercātōrem** laudāvērunt.   *The sailors praised the merchant.*

In each of these examples, the person who has something done to him or her is indicated in Latin by the *accusative singular*.

2 In Stage 8, you have met sentences like these:

amīcus **puellās** salūtat.   *The friend greets the girls.*
dominus **servōs** vituperābat.   *The master was cursing the slaves.*
nautae **mercātōrēs** laudāvērunt.   *The sailors praised the merchants.*

In these examples, the people who have something done to them are indicated in Latin by the *accusative plural*.

3 You have now met the following forms:

SINGULAR		PLURAL	
NOMINATIVE	ACCUSATIVE	NOMINATIVE	ACCUSATIVE
puella	puellam	puellae	puellās
servus	servum	servī	servōs
mercātor	mercātōrem	mercātōrēs	mercātōrēs
leō	leōnem	leōnēs	leōnēs

4 Further examples for study and translation:

1 agricola gladiātōrem laudāvit. agricola gladiātōrēs laudāvit.
2 servus agricolam interfēcit. servus agricolās interfēcit.
3 centuriō servōs laudāvit.
4 puer āctōrēs ad theātrum dūxit.
5 senex āctōrem ad forum dūxit.
6 amīcus fābulās nārrāvit.
7 amīcī ancillam salūtāvērunt.
8 agricolae nūntiōs audīvērunt.

When you have read this passage, answer the questions at the end.

vēnātiō

postquam rētiāriī ex arēnā discessērunt, tuba iterum sonuit. subitō
multī cervī arēnam intrāvērunt. cervī per tōtam arēnam currēbant,
quod perterritī erant. tum canēs ferōcēs per portam intrāvērunt.
canēs statim cervōs perterritōs agitāvērunt et interfēcērunt.
postquam canēs cervōs superāvērunt, lupī arēnam intrāvērunt.   5
lupī, quod valdē ēsuriēbant, canēs ferōciter petīvērunt. canēs erant
fortissimī, sed lupī facile canēs superāvērunt.

    Nūcerīnī erant laetissimī et Rēgulum laudābant. Pompēiānī
tamen nōn erant contentī, sed clāmābant, "ubi sunt leōnēs? cūr
Rēgulus aprōs et leōnēs retinet?"   10

    Rēgulus, postquam hunc clāmōrem audīvit, signum dedit. statim
trēs leōnēs per portam ruērunt. tuba iterum sonuit. bēstiāriī arēnam
audācissimē intrāvērunt. leōnēs tamen bēstiāriōs nōn petīvērunt.
leōnēs in arēnā recubuērunt. leōnēs obdormīvērunt!

    tum Pompēiānī erant īrātissimī, quod Rēgulus spectāculum   15
rīdiculum ēdēbat. Pompēiānī Rēgulum et Nūcerīnōs ex
amphitheātrō agitāvērunt. Nūcerīnī per viās fugiēbant, quod valdē
timēbant. Pompēiānī tamen gladiōs suōs dēstrīnxērunt et multōs
Nūcerīnōs interfēcērunt. ecce! sanguis nōn in arēnā sed per viās
fluēbat.   20

Words and Phrases

iterum	*again*	obdormīvērunt	*went to sleep*
ēsuriēbant	*were hungry*	īrātissimī	*very angry*
fortissimī	*very brave*	rīdiculum	*ridiculous, silly*
retinet	*is holding back*	ēdēbat	*was presenting*
hunc	*this*	fugiēbant	*began to flee*
trēs	*three*	suōs	*their*
audācissimē	*very boldly*	dēstrīnxērunt	*drew*
recubuērunt	*lay down*		

Wall-painting showing the great riot (see page 130)

Questions

1 What happened when the trumpet sounded?
2 When did the wolves enter the arena?
3 What was the attitude of the citizens of Pompeii to the first part of the show?
4 What did Regulus do?
5 What went wrong with the show?
6 Why did the Pompeians attack the citizens of Nuceria?
7 What made this riot so serious?

pāstor et leō

ōlim pāstor in silvā ambulābat. subitō pāstor leōnem cōnspexit. leō
tamen pāstōrem nōn agitāvit. leō lacrimābat! pāstor, postquam
leōnem cōnspexit, erat attonitus et rogāvit,
    "cūr lacrimās, leō? cūr mē nōn agitās? cūr mē nōn cōnsūmis?"
    leō trīstis pedem ostendit. pāstor spīnam in pede cōnspexit, tum   5
clāmāvit,
    "ego spīnam videō! spīnam ingentem videō! nunc intellegō! tū
lacrimās, quod pēs dolet."
    pāstor, quod benignus et fortis erat, ad leōnem cautē vēnit et
spīnam īnspexit. leō fremuit, quod ignāvus erat.   10
    "leō!" exclāmāvit pāstor, "ego perterritus sum, quod tū fremis.
sed tē adiuvō. ecce! spīna!"
    postquam hoc dīxit, pāstor spīnam quam celerrimē extrāxit. leō
ignāvus iterum fremuit et ē silvā festīnāvit.
    posteā, Rōmānī hunc pāstōrem comprehendērunt, quod   15
Chrīstiānus erat, et eum ad arēnam dūxērunt. postquam arēnam
intrāvit, pāstor spectātōrēs vīdit et valdē timēbat. tum pāstor
bēstiās vīdit et clāmāvit, "nunc mortuus sum! videō leōnēs et lupōs.
ēheu!"
    tum ingēns leō ad eum ruit. leō, postquam pāstōrem olfēcit, nōn   20
eum cōnsūmpsit sed lambēbat! pāstor attonitus leōnem agnōvit et
dīxit,
    "tē agnōscō! tū es leō trīstis! spīna erat in pede tuō."
    leō iterum fremuit, et pāstōrem ex arēnā ad salūtem dūxit.

Words and Phrases

attonitus	astonished		extrāxit	pulled out
trīstis	sad		posteā	afterwards
pedem	foot, paw		comprehendērunt	arrested
ostendit	showed		olfēcit	smelled, sniffed
spīnam	thorn		lambēbat	began to lick
dolet	hurts		agnōvit	recognized
benignus	kind		ad salūtem	to safety
fremuit	roared			
ignāvus	cowardly			
exclāmāvit	shouted		## Names and Proper Adjectives	
adiuvō	help			
hoc	this		Chrīstiānus	Christian

Practicing the Language

1 Complete each sentence with the most suitable word from the list below, and then translate it.

ego, tū, amīcōs, leōnēs, vēndō, spectās

1 . . . . . multās vīllās habeō.
2 ego servōs . . . . . .
3 tū gladiātōrēs . . . . . .
4 ego . . . . . salūtō.
5 . . . . . ancillās laudās.
6 tū . . . . . agitās.

2 Complete each sentence with the right word, and then translate it.

1 tū es vēnālīcius; tū servōs in forō . . . . . . (vēndō, vēndis, vēndit)
2 ego sum gladiātor; ego in arēnā . . . . . . (pugnō, pugnās, pugnat)
3 Fēlīx est lībertus; Fēlīx cum Caeciliō . . . . . . (cēnō, cēnās, cēnat)
4 ego multōs spectātōrēs in amphitheātrō . . . . . . (videō, vidēs, videt)
5 tū in vīllā magnificā . . . . . . (habitō, habitās, habitat)
6 Rēgulus hodiē diem nātālem . . . . . . (celebrō, celebrās, celebrat)
7 tū saepe ad amphitheātrum . . . . . . (veniō, venīs, venit)
8 ego rem . . . . . . (intellegō, intellegis, intellegit)

About the Language

1 Study the following pairs of sentences:

Pompēiānī erant īrātī.
The Pompeians were angry.

Pompēiānī erant **īrātissimī.**
The Pompeians were very angry.

Pugnāx est nōtus.
Pugnax is famous.

Pugnāx est **nōtissimus.**
Pugnax is very famous.

Grumiō erat laetus.
Grumio was happy.

Grumiō erat **laetissimus.**
Grumio was very happy.

The words in boldface are known as *superlatives*. Notice how they are translated in the examples above.

2 Further examples:

1 mercātor est trīstis. senex est trīstissimus.
2 canis erat ferōx. leō erat ferōcissimus.
3 amīcus fābulam longissimam nārrāvit.
4 murmillōnēs erant fortēs, sed rētiāriī erant fortissimī.

3 A few superlatives are formed in a different way:

mōns est pulcher. mōns Vesuvius est **pulcherrimus.**
The mountain is beautiful. *Mount Vesuvius is very beautiful.*

Gladiatorial Shows

Among the most popular entertainments in all parts of the Roman world were shows in which gladiators fought each other. These contests were held in an amphitheater. This was a large oval building, without a roof, in which rising tiers of seats surrounded an arena. Canvas awnings, supported by ropes and pulleys, were spread over part of the seating area to give shelter from the sun. The amphitheater at Pompeii was large enough to contain the whole population as well as many visitors from nearby towns. Spectators paid no admission fee as the shows were given by wealthy individuals at their own expense.

Among the many advertisements for gladiatorial shows that are to be seen painted on the walls of buildings is this one:

"Twenty pairs of gladiators, given by Lucretius Satrius Valens, priest of Nero, and ten pairs of gladiators provided by his son will fight at Pompeii from 8 to 12 April. There will also be an animal hunt. Awnings will be provided."

Soon after dawn on the day of a show, the spectators would begin to take their places. A trumpet blared and priests came out to perform the religious ceremony with which the games began. Then the gladiators entered in procession, paraded around the arena and saluted the president of the show. The gladiators were then paired off to fight each other and the contests began.

The gladiators were usually slaves or condemned criminals; they lived and trained in a school or barracks under the supervision of a professional trainer. They were not all armed in the same way. Some, who were known as Samnites, carried an oblong shield and a short sword; others, known as Thracians, had a round shield and a sword or dagger. Another type of gladiator armed with sword and shield wore a helmet with a crest shaped like a fish; the Greek name for the fish was "mormillos" and the gladiator was known as a **murmillō**. The **murmillōnēs** were often matched against the **rētiāriī** who were armed with **rētia** (*nets*) and three-pronged tridents. Other types of gladiator fought with spears, on horseback, or from chariots.

Part of the program of one particular show, together with details of the results, reads as follows:

A Thracian versus a Murmillo
won: Pugnax from Nero's school: 3 times a winner
died: Murranus from Nero's school: 3 times a winner

A Heavily-armed Gladiator versus a Thracian
won: Cycnus from the school of Julius: 8 times a winner
set free: Atticus from the school of Julius: 14 times a winner

Chariot Fighters
won: Scylax from the school of Julius: 26 times a winner
set free: Publius Ostorius: 51 times a winner

The fight ended with the death or surrender of one of the gladiators. The illustrations above, taken from the tomb of a wealthy Pompeian, show the defeated gladiator appealing to the spectators; the victor stands by ready to kill him if they decide that he deserves to die. Notice the arm raised in appeal. The spectators indicated their wishes by turning their thumbs up or down; probably turning the thumb up towards the chest meant "kill him," while turning it down meant "let him live." The final decision for death or mercy was made by the president of the games. It was not unusual for the life of the loser to be spared, especially if he were a well-known gladiator with a good number of victories to his credit. The most successful gladiators were great favorites with the crowd and received gifts of money from their admirers. One popular Pompeian gladiator was described as **suspīrium puellārum**: *the girls' heart-throb.* Eventually, if a gladiator survived long enough or showed great skill and courage, he would be awarded the wooden sword. This was a high honor and meant he would not have to fight again.

Many shows also offered a **vēnātiō**, a hunt of wild animals. The **bēstiae** (*wild beasts*) were released from cages into the arena, where they were hunted by specially trained beast-fighters called **bēstiāriī**. In the relief opposite you can see lions and a bear.

The hunters, who wore light clothing, relied upon a thrusting spear and nimble feet. By the end of the hunt all the animals and occasionally a few hunters had been killed, and their bodies were dragged out from the sandy floor of the arena to be disposed of.

The great riot in the amphitheater (based on the wall-painting shown on p. 124)

The Riot at Pompeii

The story told in this Stage is based on an actual event which occurred in A.D. 59 and is described by the Roman historian Tacitus in these words:

"About this time, a slight incident led to a serious outburst of rioting between the peoples of Pompeii and Nuceria. It occurred at a show of gladiators, sponsored by Livineius Regulus. While hurling insults at each other, in the usual manner of country people, they suddenly began to throw stones as well. Finally, they drew swords and attacked each other. The men of Pompeii won the fight. As a result, most of the families of Nuceria lost a father or a son. Many of the wounded were taken to Rome, where the Emperor Nero requested the Senate to hold an investigation. After the investigation, the Senate forbade the Pompeians to hold such shows for ten years. Livineius and others who had encouraged the riot were sent into exile."

Words and Phrases Checklist

agitat	*chases, hunts*	porta	*gate*
cōnsūmit	*eats*	postulat	*demands*
dūcit	*leads*	puer	*boy*
eum	*him*	pugnat	*fights*
facile	*easily*	recumbit	*lies down, reclines*
ferōx	*fierce, ferocious*	saepe	*often*
gladius	*sword*	sanguis	*blood*
habitat	*lives*	silva	*woods, forest*
hic	*this*	spectāculum	*show, spectacle*
ignāvus	*cowardly* (also *lazy* in other contexts)	statim	*at once*
		tōtus	*whole*
incitat	*urges on, encourages*	tuba	*trumpet*
nūntius	*messenger*	vēnātiō	*hunt*
pēs	*foot, paw*		

Word Search

Match each definition with one of the words given below.

agitation, incite, inhabit, repugnant, sanguinary, spectacular, total

1 . . . . . : offensive, repulsive
2 . . . . . : to dwell in or on
3 . . . . . : bloodthirsty
4 . . . . . : arousing interest or attention, sensational
5 . . . . . : excitement or alarm
6 . . . . . : entire
7 . . . . . : to encourage or provoke

Caldarium from the Forum Baths, Pompeii

Stage 9

thermae

Quīntus ad thermās vēnit.

Quīntus servō pecūniam dedit.

amīcī Quīntum laetē salūtāvērunt,
quod diem nātālem celebrābat.

Quīntus discum novum ferēbat.
Quīntus amīcīs discum ostendit.

postquam Quīntus discum ēmīsit,
discus statuam percussit.

ēheu! statua nāsum frāctum
habēbat.

Metella et Melissa in forō
ambulābant.
Metella fīliō dōnum quaerēbat.

fēminae mercātōrem
cōnspexērunt. mercātor
fēminīs togās ostendit.

Metella Quīntō togam ēlēgit.
Melissa mercātōrī pecūniam
dedit.

Grumiō cēnam optimam in culīnā parābat.
coquus Quīntō cēnam parābat, quod diem nātālem celebrābat.

multī hospitēs cum Quīntō cēnābant.
Clēmēns hospitibus vīnum offerēbat.

ancilla triclīnium intrāvit.
Quīntus ancillae signum dedit.
ancilla suāviter cantāvit.

thermae

cīvēs Pompēiānī trēs thermās habēbant. cīvēs cotīdiē ad thermās ībant. servī post dominōs ambulābant. servī oleum et strigilēs ferēbant.

cīvēs et servī, postquam thermās intrāvērunt, āthlētās et pugilēs vidēbant. āthlētae in palaestrā sē exercēbant. multī saliēbant, multī discōs ēmittēbant. servī cīvibus discōs quaerēbant. servī, postquam discōs invēnērunt, ad cīvēs reveniēbant. tum servī cīvibus discōs trādēbant.

cīvēs, postquam sē exercuērunt, apodytērium intrābant. omnēs in apodytēriō togās dēpōnēbant, et tepidārium intrābant. cīvēs in tepidāriō paulīsper sedēbant, tum ad caldārium ībant. in caldāriō erant multae sellae. ibi dominī sedēbant et garriēbant. servī dominīs oleum et strigilēs ferēbant. servī dominōs dīligenter rādēbant. thermae Pompēiānōs valdē dēlectābant.

Words and Phrases

thermae	baths	discōs ēmittēbant	were throwing the discus
ībant	used to go	invēnērunt	found
oleum	oil	apodytērium	changing room
strigilēs	strigils, scrapers	togās	togas
ferēbant	used to carry	tepidārium	warm room
āthlētās	athletes	paulīsper	for a short time
pugilēs	boxers	caldārium	hot room
in palaestrā	in the palaestra	ibi	there
sē exercēbant	were exercising	garriēbant	gossiped
		rādēbant	scraped

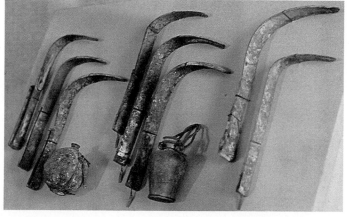

Strigils and oil pots

When you have read this story, answer the questions at the end.

in palaestrā

Caecilius Quīntō discum dedit, quod diem nātālem celebrābat. tum
Caecilius fīlium ad thermās dūxit, ubi palaestra erat. servus Quīntō
discum ferēbat.

   Caecilius et fīlius, postquam thermās intrāvērunt, ad palaestram
contendērunt. turba ingēns in palaestrā erat. Quīntus multōs   5
iuvenēs, āthlētās, pugilēs cōnspexit. Quīntus multās statuās in
palaestrā vīdit.

   "Pompēiānī āthlētīs nōtissimīs statuās posuērunt," inquit
Caecilius.

   in palaestrā erat porticus ingēns. spectātōrēs in porticū stābant.   10
servī spectātōribus vīnum offerēbant.

   Quīntus turbam prope porticum vīdit. āthlēta ingēns in mediā
turbā stābat.

   "quis est āthlēta ille?" rogāvit Quīntus.

   "ille est Milō, āthlēta nōtissimus," respondit Caecilius.   15

   Caecilius et Quīntus ad Milōnem contendērunt.

   Quīntus āthlētae discum novum ostendit. Milō, postquam
discum īnspexit, ad mediam palaestram prōcessit. āthlēta
palaestram circumspectāvit et discum ēmīsit. discus longē per aurās
ēvolāvit. spectātōrēs āthlētam laudāvērunt. servus Milōnī discum   20
quaesīvit. servus, postquam discum invēnit, ad Milōnem rediit.
servus āthlētae discum offerēbat. āthlēta tamen discum nōn accēpit.

   "discus nōn est meus," inquit Milō.

   servus Quīntō discum trādidit. tum iuvenis quoque discum
ēmīsit. discus iterum per aurās ēvolāvit. discus tamen statuam   25
percussit.

   "ēheu!" clāmāvit Caecilius. "statua nāsum frāctum habet."

   Quīntus rīdēbat. Pompēiānī rīdēbant. Milō tamen nōn rīdēbat.

   "cūr tū nōn rīdēs?" rogāvit iuvenis.

   Milō erat īrātissimus.   30

   "pestis!" respondit āthlēta. "mea est statua!"

Words and Phrases

statuās	*statues*	per aurās ⎫	⎰ *flew through*
posuērunt	*have placed, have put up*	ēvolāvit ⎭	⎱ *the air*
porticus	*colonnade*	rediit	*came back*
offerēbant	*were offering*	nōn accēpit	*did not accept*
in mediā turbā	*in the middle of the crowd*	trādidit	*handed over*
novum	*new*	percussit	*struck*
longē	*far*	nāsum frāctum	*a broken nose*

Questions

1 Why did Caecilius give Quintus a discus?
2 Where did Caecilius and Quintus go?
3 What did Quintus see in the palaestra?
4 Why were the statues in the palaestra?
5 What happened when Milo threw the discus?
6 What happened when Quintus threw it?
7 What sort of person do you think Milo was?

The palaestra in Pompeii

About the Language

1 Study the following examples:

iuvenis **servō** pecūniam trādidit.
The young man handed over money to the slave.

dominus **mercātōrī** statuam ēmit.
The master bought a statue for the merchant.

Clēmēns **puellae** vīnum offerēbat.
Clemens was offering wine to the girl.

Quīntus **amīcīs** discum ostendit.
Quintus showed the discus to his friends.

servī **leōnibus** cibum dedērunt.
The slaves gave food to the lions.

The words in boldface are in the *dative* case.

2 You have now met three cases. Notice the different ways in which they are used:

NOMINATIVE **servus** dormiēbat. *The slave was sleeping.*
ACCUSATIVE dominus **servum** excitāvit. *The master woke the slave.*
DATIVE dominus **servō** signum dedit. *The master gave a sign to the slave.*

3 Compare the nominative singular with the dative singular and dative plural in each declension:

	NOMINATIVE SINGULAR	DATIVE SINGULAR	DATIVE PLURAL
FIRST DECLENSION	puella	puellae	puellīs
SECOND DECLENSION	servus	servō	servīs
THIRD DECLENSION	mercātor	mercātōrī	mercātōribus

4 Further examples:

1 ancilla dominō cibum ostendit.
2 servus Metellae togam trādidit.
3 mercātor gladiātōribus tunicās offerēbat.
4 agricola uxōrī ānulum ēmit.

5 Notice the different cases of the words for *I* and *you*:

NOMINATIVE	ACCUSATIVE	DATIVE
ego	mē	mihi
tū	tē	tibi

ego senem salūtō.	*I greet the old man.*
senex **mē** salūtat.	*The old man greets me.*
senex **mihi** statuam ostendit.	*The old man shows a statue to me.*
tū pictūram pingis.	*You are painting a picture.*
āthlēta **tē** laudat.	*The athlete praises you.*
āthlēta **tibi** pecūniam dat.	*The athlete gives money to you.*

Storefronts

in tabernā

Metella et Melissa ē vīllā māne discessērunt. Metella fīliō togam quaerēbat. Metella et ancilla, postquam forum intrāvērunt, tabernam cōnspexērunt, ubi togae optimae erant. multae fēminae erant in tabernā. servī fēminīs stolās ostendēbant. duo gladiātōrēs quoque in tabernā erant. servī gladiātōribus tunicās ostendēbant.   5

māne   *in the morning*

mercātor in mediā tabernā stābat. mercātor erat Marcellus. Marcellus, postquam Metellam vīdit, rogāvit,

"quid quaeris, domina?"

"togam quaerō," inquit Metella. "ego fīliō dōnum quaerō, quod diem nātālem celebrat." 10

"ego multās togās habeō," respondit mercātor.

mercātor servīs signum dedit. servī mercātōrī togās celeriter trādidērunt. Marcellus fēminīs togās ostendit. Metella et ancilla togās īnspexērunt.

"hercle!" clāmāvit Melissa. "hae togae sunt sordidae." 15

Marcellus servōs vituperābat.

"sunt intus togae splendidae," inquit Marcellus.

Marcellus fēminās intus dūxit. mercātor fēminīs aliās togās ostendit. Metella Quīntō mox togam splendidam ēlēgit.

"haec toga, quantī est?" rogāvit Metella. 20

"quīnquāgintā dēnāriōs cupiō," respondit Marcellus.

"quīnquāgintā dēnāriōs cupis! furcifer!" clāmāvit Melissa. "ego tibi decem dēnāriōs offerō."

"quadrāgintā dēnāriōs cupiō," respondit mercātor.

"tibi quīndecim dēnāriōs offerō," inquit ancilla. 25

"quid? haec est toga pulcherrima! quadrāgintā dēnāriōs cupiō," respondit Marcellus.

"tū nimium postulās," inquit Metella. "ego tibi trīgintā dēnāriōs dō."

"cōnsentiō," respondit Marcellus. 30

Melissa Marcellō pecūniam dedit. Marcellus Metellae togam trādidit.

"ego tibi grātiās maximās agō, domina," inquit Marcellus.

Words and Phrases

domina	*madam*	quīnquāgintā dēnāriōs	*fifty denarii*
dōnum	*present, gift*	cupiō	*I want*
hae togae	*these togas*	decem	*ten*
sordidae	*dirty*	quadrāgintā	*forty*
intus	*inside*	quīndecim	*fifteen*
aliās	*other*	nimium	*too much*
ēlēgit	*chose*	trīgintā	*thirty*
haec	*this*	cōnsentiō	*I agree*
quantī est?	*how much is it?*	ego … grātiās … agō	*I thank, give thanks*

Practicing the Language

1 Complete each sentence with a word that makes good sense, and then translate it.

> for example: mercātōrēs fēminīs tunicās . . . . . . (audīvērunt, ostendērunt, timuērunt)
>
> mercātōrēs fēminīs tunicās ostendērunt.
> *The merchants showed the tunics to the women.*

1 ancilla dominō vīnum . . . . . . (timuit, dedit, salūtāvit)
2 iuvenis puellae stolam . . . . . . (ēmit, vēnit, prōcessit)
3 fēminae servīs tunicās . . . . . . (intrāvērunt, quaesīvērunt, contendērunt)
4 cīvēs āctōrī pecūniam . . . . . . (laudāvērunt, vocāvērunt, trādidērunt)
5 centuriō mercātōribus decem dēnāriōs . . . . . . (trādidit, ēmit, vīdit)

2 Complete each sentence with the right word, and then translate it.

> for example: gladiātōrēs amīcīs togās . . . . . . (ostendit, ostendērunt)
>
> gladiātōrēs amīcīs togās ostendērunt.
> *The gladiators showed the togas to their friends.*

1 puella gladiātōribus tunicās . . . . . . (dedit, dedērunt)
2 cīvēs Milōnī statuam . . . . . . (posuit, posuērunt)
3 mercātor amīcō vīnum . . . . . . (trādidit, trādidērunt)
4 coquus ancillae ānulum . . . . . . (ēmit, ēmērunt)
5 vēnālīciī fēminīs servōs . . . . . . (ostendit, ostendērunt)
6 servus Quīntō discum . . . . . . (quaesīvit, quaesīvērunt)
7 nautae uxōribus stolās pulchrās . . . . . . (ēlēgit, ēlēgērunt)
8 Clēmēns et Grumiō Metellae cēnam optimam . . . . . . (parāvit, parāvērunt)

3 This exercise is based on the story "in tabernā," on pages 141-42. Read the story again. Complete each of the sentences below with the right word or phrase, and then translate it.

1 Metella . . . . . . ad forum ambulāvit. (cum Quīntō, cum Grumiōne, cum Melissā)
2 postquam forum intrāvērunt, ... cōnspexērunt. (portum, tabernam, vīllam)
3 Metella gladiātōrēs et . . . . . . in tabernā vīdit. (āctōrēs, fēminās, centuriōnēs)
4 servī fēminīs . . . . . . ostendēbant. (tunicās, stolās, togās)
5 servī gladiātōribus . . . . . . ostendēbant. (togās, stolās, tunicās)
6 mercātor servīs . . . . . . dedit. (signum, togam, gladium)
7 servī mercātōrī . . . . . . trādidērunt. (togam, togās, stolās)
8 mercātor . . . . . . vituperāvit, quod togae erant sordidae. (gladiātōrēs, fēminās, servōs)

Apodyterium at the Stabian Baths, Pompeii

duo servī in apodytēriō stant. servī sunt Sceledrus et Anthrāx.

Sceledrus: cūr nōn labōrās, Anthrāx? num dormīs?

Anthrāx: quid dīcis? dīligenter labōrō. ego cīvibus togās custōdiō.

Sceledrus: togās custōdīs? mendāx es!

Anthrāx: cūr mē vituperās? mendāx nōn sum. togās custōdiō.   5

Sceledrus: tē vituperō, quod fūr est in apodytēriō, sed tū nihil facis.

Anthrāx: ubi est fūr? fūrem nōn videō.

Sceledrus: ecce! homō ille est fūr. fūrem facile agnōscō.

           (Sceledrus Anthrācī fūrem ostendit. fūr togam suam dēpōnit et

           togam splendidam induit. servī ad fūrem statim currunt.)   10

Anthrāx: quid facis? furcifer! haec toga nōn est tua!

fūr: mendāx es! mea est toga! abī!

Sceledrus: tē agnōscō! pauper es, sed togam splendidam geris.

           (mercātor intrat. togam frūstrā quaerit.)

mercātor: ēheu! ubi est toga mea? toga ēvānuit!   15

           (mercātor circumspectat.)

           ecce! hic fūr togam meam gerit!

fūr: parce! parce! pauperrimus sum . . . uxor mea est aegra

           . . . decem līberōs habeō . . .

mercātor et servī fūrem nōn audiunt, sed eum ad iūdicem trahunt.   20

Words and Phrases

induit	*is putting on*
abī!	*go away!*
pauper	*a poor man*
geris	*you are wearing*
parce!	*mercy!*
aegra	*sick, ill*
līberōs	*children*

The Baths

About the middle of the afternoon, Caecilius would make his way, with a group of friends, to the public baths. These were not just swimming pools but something more like a modern health club. Let us imagine that Caecilius decides to visit the baths situated just to the north of the forum, and let us follow him through the various rooms and activities.

At one of the entrances, he pays a small admission fee to the **ōstiārius** (*doorkeeper*) and then goes to the **palaestra** (*exercise area*). This is an open space surrounded by a colonnade, rather like a large peristylium. Here he spends a little time greeting other friends and taking part in some of the popular exercises, which included throwing a large ball from one to another, wrestling, and fencing with wooden swords. These games were not taken too seriously, but were a pleasant preparation for the bath which followed.

From the palaestra, Caecilius and his friends walk along a passage into a large hall known as the **apodytērium** (*changing-room*). Here they remove all their clothes and hand them to one of the slave attendants, who places them in niches arranged in rows along the wall. Leaving the apodyterium, they pass through an arched doorway into the **tepidārium** (*warm room*) and there spend a little time sitting on benches around the wall in a warm steamy atmosphere, perspiring gently and getting their bodies ready for the higher temperatures in the next room. This is the **caldārium** (*hot room*). At one end of the caldarium there was a large marble bath, oblong in shape, and stretching across the full width of the room. This bath was filled with hot water in which the bathers sat or wallowed. The Romans did not have soap, but used olive oil instead. After soaking in the bath, Caecilius summons a slave to rub him down with the oil that he has brought with him in a little pot. For this rubbing down, Caecilius lies on a marble slab while the slave works the oil into his skin, and then gently removes it and the impurities with a blunt metal scraper known as a strigil. Next comes the masseur, to massage skin and muscles. Refreshed by this treatment, Caecilius then goes to the large stone tub at the other end of the caldarium for a dip in cold water.

Before dressing again he might well visit the **frigidārium** (*cold room*), and there take a plunge in a deep circular pool of unheated water, followed by a brisk rub-down with his towel.

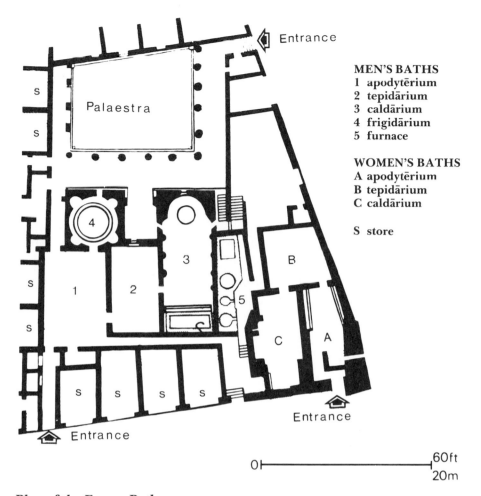

MEN'S BATHS
1 apodytērium
2 tepidārium
3 caldārium
4 frigidārium
5 furnace

WOMEN'S BATHS
A apodytērium
B tepidārium
C caldārium

S store

Palaestra

Entrance

Entrance

Entrance

0   60ft
     20m

Plan of the Forum Baths

The Roman taking his bath did not hurry, nor did he take it quietly. He liked the company of his friends, and he was not shy about expressing his enjoyment. Here is a description of the sounds that could be heard, written by Seneca, who lived in Rome uncomfortably close to a set of baths.

"I am surrounded by uproar. My apartment is over a set of baths. Just imagine the babel of sounds that strike my ears. When the athletic gentlemen below are exercising themselves, lifting lead weights, I can hear their grunts. I can hear the whistling of their breath as it escapes from their lungs. I can hear somebody enjoying a cheap rub-down and the smack of the masseur's hands on his shoulders. If his hand comes down flat, it makes one sound; if it comes down hollowed, it makes another. Add to this the noise of a brawler or pickpocket being arrested down below, the racket made by the man who likes to sing in his bath, or the sound of enthusiasts who hurl themselves into the water with a tremendous splash. Next, I can hear the screech of the hair-plucker, who advertises himself by shouting. He is never quiet except when he is plucking hair and making his victim shout instead. Finally, just imagine the cries of the cake-seller, the sausage-man, and the other food-sellers as they advertise their goods around the bath, all adding to the din."

Clearly this was more than just a place to get clean in. It was much more like a popular social club.

The Romans were not the first people to build public baths. This was one of the many things they learned from the Greeks. But with their engineering skill the Romans greatly improved the methods of heating them. The previous method had been to heat the water in tanks over a furnace and to stand charcoal burners in the warm room and the hot room to keep up the air temperature. The charcoal burners were not very efficient and they failed to heat the floor.

In the first century B.C., a Roman invented the first central heating system. The furnace was placed below the floor level; the floor was supported on small brick piles, leaving space through which hot air from the furnace could circulate. In this way, the floor was warmed from below. The hot bath was placed near the furnace, and a steady temperature was maintained by the hot air passing immediately below. Later, flues were placed in the walls and warm air from beneath the floor was drawn up through them. This ingenious heating system was known

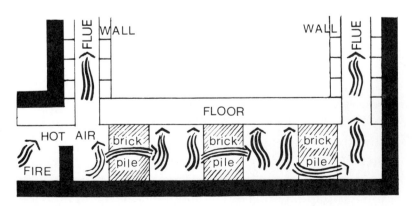

Cross-section of hypocaust

as a hypocaust. It was used not only in baths but also in private houses, particularly in the colder parts of the Roman empire, such as Britain. Charcoal was the fuel most commonly burned in the furnaces.

A hypocaust viewed from above

Words and Phrases Checklist

agnōscit	*recognizes*	īnspicit	*looks at, inspects,*
celebrat	*celebrates*		*examines*
celeriter	*quickly*	iterum	*again*
cīvis	*citizen*	manet	*remains, stays*
cupit	*wants*	medius	*middle*
dat	*gives*	mox	*soon*
dedit	*gave*	nōtus	*well known, famous*
diēs	*day*	offert	*offers*
diēs nātālis	*birthday*	ostendit	*shows*
ēmittit	*throws, sends out*	paulīsper	*for a short time*
exercet	*exercises*	post	*after*
fert	*brings, carries*	revenit	*comes back, returns*
homō	*person, man*	suus	*his*
hospes	*guest*	trādit	*hands over*
ille	*that*		

Word Search

Match each definition with one of the words given below.

civilization, emit, exercise, homicide, hospital, ostensible, reiterate

1 . . . . . : seeming; apparent
2 . . . . . : to give off or send out
3 . . . . . : to repeat
4 . . . . . : human society
5 . . . . . : murder
6 . . . . . : to engage in vigorous physical activity
7 . . . . . : a building used to house and treat sick persons

rhētor

Rōmānus dīcit,
    "nōs Rōmānī sumus architectī. nōs viās et pontēs aedificāmus."

"nōs Rōmānī sumus agricolae. nōs fundōs optimōs habēmus."

Graecus dīcit,
    "nōs Graecī sumus sculptōrēs. nōs statuās pulchrās facimus."

"nōs Graecī sumus pictōrēs. nōs pictūrās pingimus."

Rōmānus dīcit,
  "vōs Graecī estis ignāvī. vōs āctōrēs semper spectātis."

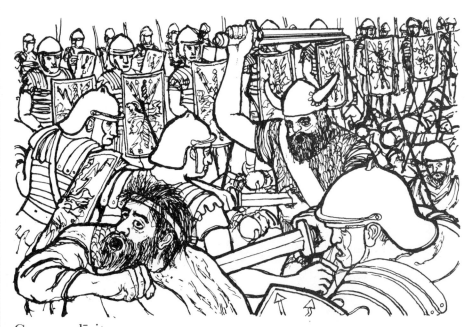

Graecus dīcit,
  "vōs Rōmānī estis barbarī. vōs semper pugnātis."

Rōmānus dīcit,
  "nōs sumus callidī. nōs rēs ūtilēs facimus."

Graecus dīcit,
  "nōs sumus callidiōrēs quam vōs. nōs Graecī Rōmānōs docēmus."

Bridge over the River Tagus, near Alcantara, Spain

contrōversia

Quīntus amīcum Graecum habēbat. amīcus erat Alexander.
Quīntus et Alexander ad palaestram ībant, ubi rhētor Graecus erat.
hic rhētor erat Theodōrus et prope palaestram habitābat. in
palaestrā erat porticus longa, ubi Theodōrus iuvenēs docēbat.
postquam ad hanc porticum vēnērunt, Alexander et Quīntus   5
rhētorem audīvērunt. rhētor iuvenibus contrōversiam nūntiāvit,
"Graecī sunt meliōrēs quam Rōmānī."

    Quīntus vehementer exclāmāvit,

    "minimē! nōs Rōmānī sumus meliōrēs quam Graecī."

    Theodōrus, postquam hanc sententiam audīvit, respondit,   10

    "haec est tua sententia. nōs tamen nōn sententiam quaerimus,
nōs argūmentum quaerimus."

    tum Quīntus rhētorī et amīcīs argūmentum explicāvit.

"nōs Rōmānī sumus fortissimī. nōs barbarōs ferōcissimōs superāmus. nōs imperium maximum habēmus. nōs pācem servāmus. vōs Graecī semper contentiōnēs habētis. vōs semper estis turbulentī.

"nōs sumus architectī optimī. nōs viās et pontēs ubīque aedificāmus. urbs Rōma est maior quam omnēs urbēs.

"postrēmō nōs Rōmānī dīligenter labōrāmus. deī igitur nōbīs imperium maximum dant. vōs Graecī estis ignāvī. vōs numquam labōrātis. deī vōbīs nihil dant."

postquam Quīntus hanc sententiam explicāvit, iuvenēs Pompēiānī vehementer plausērunt et eum laudāvērunt. deinde Alexander surrēxit. iuvenēs Pompēiānī tacuērunt et Alexandrum intentē spectāvērunt.

"vōs Rōmānī estis miserandī. vōs imperium maximum habētis, sed vōs estis imitātōrēs; nōs Graecī sumus auctōrēs. vōs Graecās statuās spectātis, vōs Graecōs librōs legitis, Graecōs rhētorēs audītis. vōs Rōmānī estis rīdiculī, quod estis Graeciōrēs quam nōs Graecī!"

iuvenēs, postquam Alexander sententiam suam explicāvit, rīsērunt. tum Theodōrus nūntiāvit,

"Alexander victor est. argūmentum optimum explicāvit."

Words and Phrases

contrōversia	*debate*	maior quam	*greater than, bigger than*
rhētor	*teacher*	postrēmō	*lastly*
docēbat	*used to teach*	deī	*gods*
meliōrēs quam	*better than*	dant	*give*
minimē!	*no!*	ignāvī	*lazy*
sententiam	*opinion*	deinde	*then*
argūmentum	*proof*	surrēxit	*got up*
barbarōs	*barbarians*	miserandī	*pathetic, pitiful*
imperium	*empire*	imitātōrēs	*imitators*
pācem	*peace*	auctōrēs	*creators*
architectī	*builders, architects*	librōs	*books*
pontēs	*bridges*	legitis	*read*
ubīque	*everywhere*	rīsērunt	*laughed*
aedificāmus	*build*		

Names and Proper Adjectives

Graecum	*Greek*
Graeciōrēs	*more Greek*

statuae

postquam Theodōrus Alexandrum laudāvit, iuvenēs Pompēiānī ē
porticū discessērunt. Alexander et Quīntus ad vīllam ambulābant,
ubi Alexander et duo frātrēs habitābant.

Alexander frātribus dōnum quaerēbat, quod diem nātālem
celebrābant.   5

in viā īnstitor parvās statuās vēndēbat et clāmābat:

"statuae! optimae statuae!"

Alexander frātribus statuās ēmit. statuae erant senex, iuvenis,
puella pulchra. Alexander, postquam statuās ēmit, ad vīllam cum
Quīntō contendit.   10

duo frātrēs in hortō sedēbant. Diodōrus pictūram pingēbat,
Thrasymachus librum Graecum legēbat. postquam Alexander et
Quīntus vīllam intrāvērunt, puerī ad eōs cucurrērunt. Diodōrus
statuās cōnspexit.

"Alexander, quid portās?' inquit.   15

"vōs estis fēlīcēs," inquit Alexander. "ego vōbīs dōnum habeō
quod vōs diem nātālem celebrātis. ecce!" Alexander frātribus
statuās ostendit.

"quam pulchra est puella," inquit Diodōrus. "dā mihi puellam!"

"minimē! frāter, dā mihi puellam!" clāmāvit Thrasymachus.   20
puerī dissentiēbant et lacrimābant.

"hercle! vōs estis stultissimī puerī!" clāmāvit Alexander īrātus.

"semper dissentītis, semper lacrimātis. abīte! abīte! ego statuās retineō!"

p__puerī, postquam Alexander hoc dīxit, abiērunt. Diodōrus 25
pictūram in terram dēiēcit, quod īrātus erat. Thrasymachus librum in piscīnam dēiēcit, quod īrātissimus erat.

__tum Quīntus dīxit,

__"Alexander, dā mihi statuās! Thrasymache! Diodōre! venīte hūc! Thrasymache, ecce! ego tibi senem dō, quod senex erat 30 philosophus. Diodōre, tibi iuvenem dō, quod iuvenis erat pictor. ego mihi puellam dō, quod ego sum sōlus! vōsne estis contentī?"

__"sumus contentī," respondērunt puerī.

__"ecce, Alexander," inquit Quīntus, "vōs Graeculī estis optimī artificēs sed turbulentī. nōs Rōmānī vōbīs pācem damus." 35

__"et vōs praemium accipitis," susurrāvit Thrasymachus.

Words and Phrases

frātrēs	*brothers*	in terram	*onto the ground*
īnstitor	*peddler, street-vendor*	dēiēcit	*threw*
ad eōs	*to them*	in piscīnam	*into the fishpond*
fēlīcēs	*lucky*	venīte hūc!	*come here!*
quam!	*how!*	philosophus	*philosopher*
dā!	*give!*	sōlus	*lonely*
dissentiēbant	*were arguing*	vōsne estis contentī?	*are you satisfied?*
stultissimī	*very stupid*	artificēs	*artists*
retineō	*am keeping*	praemium	*profit*
abiērunt	*went away*	susurrāvit	*whispered, mumbled*

Names and Proper Adjectives

Graeculī	*poor little Greeks*

About the Language

1 In this Stage, you have met sentences with *we* and *you*:

nōs labōrāmus. vōs labōrātis.
We work. *You work.*

nōs currimus. vōs curritis.
We run. *You run.*

Notice that **vōs labōrātis** and **vōs curritis** are *plural* forms. They are used when *you* refers to more than one person.

2 You have now met the whole of the present tense:

(ego)	portō	*I carry*
(tū)	portās	*you (singular) carry*
	portat	*s/he, it carries*
(nōs)	portāmus	*we carry*
(vōs)	portātis	*you (plural) carry*
	portant	*they carry*

3 Notice that **nōs** and **vōs** are not strictly necessary, since the endings **-mus** and **-tis** make it clear that *we* and *you* are being spoken about. The Romans normally left out **nōs** and **vōs**, just as they left out **ego** and **tū**.

4 Further examples:

1 nōs pugnāmus. vōs dormītis.
2 vōs clāmātis. nōs audīmus.
3 ambulāmus. dīcimus. vidēmus.
4 vidētis. nūntiātis. intrāmus.

5 The Latin for *we are* and *you (plural) are* is as follows:

nōs sumus iuvenēs.   vōs estis pictōrēs.
We are young men.   *You are artists.*

nōs sumus fortēs.   vōs estis ignāvī.
We are brave.   *You are cowardly.*

So the complete present tense of **sum** is:

(ego)	sum	*I am*
(tū)	es	*you (singular) are*
	est	*s/he, it is*
(nōs)	sumus	*we are*
(vōs)	estis	*you (plural) are*
	sunt	*they are*

When you have read this story, answer the questions at the end.

ānulus Aegyptius

Syphāx in tabernā sedēbat. caupō Syphācī vīnum dedit. Syphāx caupōnī ānulum trādidit.

"pecūniam nōn habeō," inquit, "quod Neptūnus nāvem meam dēlēvit."

caupō, postquam ānulum accēpit, eum īnspexit.   5

"ānulus antīquus est," inquit.

"ita vērō, antīquus est," Syphāx caupōnī respondit. "servus Aegyptius mihi ānulum dedit. servus in pȳramide ānulum invēnit."

caupō, postquam tabernam clausit, ad vīllam suam festīnāvit. caupō uxōrī ānulum ostendit. caupō uxōrī ānulum dedit, quod   10
ānulus eam dēlectāvit.

uxor postrīdiē ad urbem contendēbat. subitō servus ingēns in viā appāruit. pecūniam postulāvit. fēmina, quod erat perterrita, servō pecūniam dedit. servus ānulum cōnspexit. ānulum postulāvit. fēmina servō eum trādidit.   15

fēmina ad tabernam rediit et marītum quaesīvit. mox eum invēnit. caupō incendium spectābat. ēheu! taberna ardēbat! fēmina marītō rem tōtam nārrāvit.

"ānulus īnfēlīx est," inquit caupō. "ānulus tabernam meam dēlēvit."   20

servus ingēns, postquam pecūniam et ānulum cēpit, ad urbem contendit. subitō trēs servōs cōnspexit. servī inimīcī erant. inimīcī, postquam pecūniam cōnspexērunt, servum verberābant. servus fūgit, sed ānulum āmīsit.

Words and Phrases

caupō	*innkeeper*	ardēbat	*was on fire*
dēlēvit	*has destroyed*	īnfēlīx	*unlucky*
antīquus	*old, ancient*	āmīsit	*lost*
in pȳramide	*in a pyramid*		
clausit	*shut, closed*		
eam	*her*		
postrīdiē	*(on) the next day*		
marītum	*husband*		
incendium	*blaze, fire*		

Names and Proper Adjectives

Aegyptius	*Egyptian*
Neptūnus	*Neptune (god of the sea)*

Grumiō cum Poppaeā ambulābat. ānulum in viā invēnit.
"quid vidēs?" rogāvit Poppaea.
"ānulum videō," inquit. "ānulus Aegyptius est."
"euge!" inquit Poppaea. "ānulus fēlīx est."

Questions

1 How did Syphax pay for his drink?
2 Why did he pay for it in this way?
3 How did the innkeeper comment on what Syphax had given him?
4 Where, according to Syphax, had it come from?
5 What did the innkeeper do with the gift?
6 What happened to the innkeeper's wife?
7 What happened to the innkeeper?
8 What happened to the big slave in the city?
9 What did Grumio see in the road and what did Poppaea think of it?
10 Who have the ring at the end of the story? What do you expect to happen as a result?

Practicing the Language

1 Complete each sentence with the most suitable phrase from the list below, and then translate it.

fābulam agimus, contrōversiam habēmus, cibum offerimus,
stolās compōnimus, pānem parāmus

1 nōs sumus rhētorēs Graecī; nōs in palaestrā . . . . . .
2 nōs sumus āctōrēs nōtissimī; nōs in theātrō . . . . . .
3 nōs sumus ancillae pulchrae; nōs fēminīs . . . . . .
4 nōs sumus coquī; nōs dominīs . . . . . .
5 nōs sumus pistōrēs; nōs cīvibus . . . . . .

2 Complete each sentence with the most suitable word from the list below, and then translate it.

servī, āthlētae, pictōrēs, vēnālīciī, gladiātōrēs

1 vōs estis . . . . . callidī; vōs pictūrās magnificās pingitis.
2 vōs estis . . . . . fortēs; vōs in arēnā pugnātis.
3 nōs sumus . . . . . ; nōs in thermīs togās custōdīmus.
4 vōs servōs in forō vēnditis, quod vōs estis . . . . . .
5 nōs ad palaestram contendimus, quod nōs sumus . . . . . .

About the Language

1 Study the following pairs of sentences:

nōs Rōmānī sumus callidī.   *We Romans are clever.*
nōs Rōmānī sumus **callidiōrēs**   *We Romans are cleverer than you Greeks.*
quam vōs Graecī.

nōs Rōmānī sumus fortēs.   *We Romans are brave.*
nōs Rōmānī sumus **fortiōrēs**   *We Romans are braver than you Greeks.*
quam vōs Graecī.

The words in boldface are known as *comparatives*. They are used to compare two things or groups with each other. In the examples above, the Romans are comparing themselves with the Greeks.

2 Further examples:

1 Pompēiānī sunt stultī. Nūcerīnī sunt stultiōrēs quam Pompēiānī.
2 Diodōrus erat īrātus, sed Thrasymachus erat īrātior quam Diodōrus.
3 mea vīlla est pulchra, sed tua vīlla est pulchrior quam mea.

3 The following word forms its comparative in an unusual way:

Nūceria est magna.   *Nuceria is large.*
Rōma est **maior** quam Nūceria.   *Rome is larger than Nuceria.*

Schools

Quintus would have first gone to school when he was about seven years old. Like other Roman schools, the one that Quintus attended would have been small, and consisted of about thirty students and a teacher known as the **ludī magister**.

Parents were not obliged by law to send their children to school, and those who wanted education for their children had to pay for it. The charges were not high, and the advantages of being able to read and write were so widely appreciated that many people were prepared to pay for their sons to go to school at least for a few years. Daughters were usually educated at home, but rich people sometimes sent them to school.

On the journey between home and school, students were normally escorted by a slave known as a **paedagōgus**. Another slave carried their books and writing materials.

The materials that Quintus used for writing were rather different from ours. Frequently he wrote on **tabulae** (*wooden tablets*) coated with a thin film of wax, and he inscribed the letters on the wax surface with a thin stick of metal, bone, or ivory. This stick was called a **stilus**. The end opposite the writing point was flat so that it could be used to rub out mistakes and make the wax smooth again. Several tablets were strung together to make a little writing-book. At other times he wrote with ink on papyrus, a material that looked rather like modern paper but was rougher in texture. It was manufactured from the fibers of the papyrus reed that grew along the banks of the River Nile in Egypt. For writing on papyrus he used either a reed or a goose-quill sharpened and split at one end like the modern pen-nib. Ink was made from soot and resin or other gummy substances, forming a paste that was thinned by adding water. The best inks were so hard and durable that they are perfectly legible even today on the pieces of papyrus that have survived.

In the drawing on page 165 you see tabulae joined together, stili, inkwells and a goose-quill, and rolls of papyrus.

Pictures of scenes in school show that there were generally no desks and no blackboard. Students sat on benches or stools, resting tablets on their knees. The teacher sat on a high chair overlooking his class. Discipline was usually strict and sometimes harsh.

The school day began early and lasted for six hours with a short break

Writing materials

at noon. Holidays were given on public festivals and on every ninth day which was a market-day; during the hot summer months fewer students attended lessons, and some teachers may have closed their schools altogether from July to October.

When he was eleven, Quintus would have moved to a secondary school run by a **grammaticus**. This teacher introduced his students to the work of famous Greek and Roman writers, beginning with the *Iliad* and *Odyssey* of Homer. Then the students moved on to the tragedies of

The J. Paul Getty Museum in Malibu, California, is a replica of the Villa dei Papiri which stood outside the town of Herculaneum and was destroyed during the eruption of Vesuvius in A.D. 79.

Aeschylus, Sophocles, and Euripides, Greek playwrights who had written their plays in Athens in the fifth century B.C. The Roman poet most frequently read at school was Vergil. Besides listening to works of literature and reading them aloud, the students learned long passages by heart; many educated people could remember these passages in later life and quote or recite them. The students were also taught a little history and geography, mainly in order to understand references to famous people and places mentioned in the literature.

When he left the grammaticus at the age of fifteen or sixteen. Quintus would have a good knowledge of Greek as well as Latin. This knowledge of Greek not only introduced the students to a culture which the Romans greatly admired and which had inspired much of their own civilization, but it was also very useful because Greek was widely spoken in the countries of the eastern Mediterranean where Roman merchants and government officials frequently traveled on business.

Many children finished their schooling at the age of eleven, having learned to read, write, and do simple arithmetic. Most of those who went on to the school of the grammaticus finished at about fifteen, but a few then proceeded to a third stage. They went to a **rhētor**, like Theodorus in our story. This teacher, who was often a highly educated Greek, gave more advanced lessons in literature and trained his students in the art of public speaking. This was a very important skill for young men who expected to take part in public life. They needed it to present cases in court, to express their opinions in town board meetings, to address the people at election time, and in many other situations. The rhetor taught the rules for making different kinds of speeches and made his students practice arguing for and against a point of view. Students also learned how to vary their tone of voice and emphasize their words with gestures.

We have not so far mentioned the teaching of science and technical subjects in Roman schools. It is true that the Greeks had made important discoveries in mathematics, philosophy and some aspects of physics; it is also true that the Romans were experienced in such things as the methods of surveying and the use of concrete in building. But these things played little part in school work. The purpose of ordinary Roman schools was to teach those things which were thought to be most necessary for civilized living: the ability to read and write, a knowledge of simple arithmetic, the appreciation of fine literature, and the ability to speak and argue convincingly. Philosophy and science were taught in only a few special schools, and technical skills were learned by becoming an apprentice in a trade or business.

Words and Phrases Checklist

abit	*goes away*	nōs	*we*
accipit	*accepts*	nūntiat	*announces*
callidus	*clever, smart*	pāx	*peace*
capit	*takes*	portus	*harbor*
contentus	*satisfied*	quam	*than, how*
exclāmat	*exclaims*	semper	*always*
frāter	*brother*	sententia	*opinion*
hercle!	*by Hercules!*	servat	*saves, protects*
imperium	*empire*	sōlus	*alone, lonely*
inimīcus	*enemy*	tacet	*is silent, is quiet*
invenit	*finds*	uxor	*wife*
it	*goes*	vehementer	*violently, loudly*
liber	*book*	vōs	*you (plural)*

Word Search

Match each definition with one of the words given below.

conservation, contented, fraternal, imperial, invent, library, sentence

1 . . . . . : the act of saving or preserving
2 . . . . . : a room or building for keeping books
3 . . . . . : to create or devise
4 . . . . . : having command or authority
5 . . . . . : a judgment or verdict
6 . . . . . : brotherly
7 . . . . . : pleased, happy

Wall-painting showing free bread being distributed to bribe voters

PISTORES RVFVM II VIRVM ROGANT

candidātī

cīvēs in forō candidātōs spectant.

agricolae clāmant,
    "nōs candidātum optimum habēmus."
"candidātus noster est Lūcius."
"nōs Lūciō favēmus."

mercātōrēs agricolīs respondent,
    "nōs candidātum optimum habēmus."
"candidātus noster est mercātor."
"nōs mercātōrī favēmus."

pistōrēs in forō clāmant,
    "nōs pistōrēs candidātum optimum
      habēmus."
    "candidātus noster est pistor."
    "nōs pistōrī crēdimus."

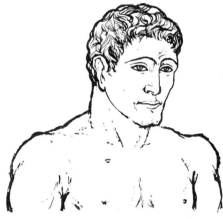

iuvenēs pistōribus respondent,
    "nōs iuvenēs candidātum optimum
      habēmus."
    "candidātus noster est āthlēta."
    "nōs āthlētae crēdimus."

fūrēs clāmant,
    "nōs quoque candidātum habēmus."
    "candidātus noster est fūr."
    "nōs candidātō nostrō nōn crēdimus
      sed favēmus."

Marcus et Quārtus

Marcus Tullius et Quārtus Tullius erant frātrēs. Marcus et Quārtus
in vīllā contentiōnem habēbant. Marcus Quārtō dīxit,
  "Āfer candidātus optimus est. Āfer multās vīllās et multās
tabernās habet. Pompēiānī Āfrō favent, quod vir dīves est."
  "minimē! Holcōnius candidātus optimus est," Quārtus frātrī   5
respondit. "Holcōnius est vir nōbilis. Pompēiānī Holcōniō crēdunt,
quod pater senātor erat."
  Quārtus, quod erat īrātissimus, ē vīllā discessit. Quārtus sibi
dīxit,
  "frāter meus est stultissimus. gēns nostra Holcōniō semper   10
favet."
  Quārtus per viam ambulābat et rem cōgitābat. subitō parvam
tabernam cōnspexit, ubi scrīptor habitābat. scrīptor Sulla erat.
Quārtus, postquam tabernam vīdit, cōnsilium cēpit. tabernam
intrāvit et Sullam ad vīllam suam invītāvit.   15
  postquam ad vīllam vēnērunt, Quārtus Sullae mūrum ostendit.
  "scrībe hunc titulum!" inquit. "scrībe 'Quārtus et frāter Holcōniō
favent. Quārtus et frāter Holcōniō crēdunt.'"
  Quārtus scrīptōrī decem dēnāriōs dedit.
  "placetne tibi?" rogāvit Quārtus.   20
  "mihi placet," Sulla Quārtō respondit. Sulla, postquam dēnāriōs
accēpit, titulum in mūrō scrīpsit.

Words and Phrases

candidātus	*candidate*	scrīptor	*sign-writer*
favent	*favor, give support to*	cōnsilium cēpit	*had an idea*
dīves	*rich*	mūrum	*wall*
vir nōbilis	*a man of noble birth*	scrībe!	*write!*
crēdunt	*trust, have faith in*	titulum	*advertisement, slogan*
sibi dīxit	*said to himself*	placetne tibi?	*does it suit you?*
gēns nostra	*our family*	scrīpsit	*wrote*
rem cōgitābat	*was considering the problem*		

Sulla

Marcus ē vīllā vēnit. Sullam vīdit. titulum cōnspexit. postquam titulum lēgit, īrātus erat. Marcus scrīptōrem valdē vituperābat.

"frāter tuus mē ad vīllam invītāvit," inquit Sulla. "frāter tuus mihi decem dēnāriōs dedit."

"frāter meus est stultior quam asinus," Marcus Sullae respondit. 5
"in vīllā nostrā ego sum dominus, quod sum senior. Sulla, crāde illam īnscrīptiōnem! scrībe titulum novum!"

Marcus Sullae quīndecim dēnāriōs dedit.

"placetne tibi?" rogāvit.

"mihi placet," Sulla Marcō respondit. Sulla, postquam 10
īnscrīptiōnem ērāsit, hunc titulum scrīpsit, "Marcus et frāter Āfrō favent. Marcus et frāter Āfrō crēdunt."

Marcus erat laetissimus et frātrem ē vīllā vocāvit. Marcus frātrī titulum novum ostendit. Quārtus, postquam titulum lēgit, īrātus erat. Quārtus Marcum pulsāvit. tum frātrēs in viā pugnābant! 15

"Marce! Quārte! dēsistite! intrō īte!" clāmāvit Sulla. "cōnsilium optimum habeō."

postquam frātrēs vīllam intrāvērunt, Sulla celeriter rem cōnfēcit. duōs titulōs in mūrō scrīpsit. tum frātrēs ē vīllā vocāvit.

scrīptor frātribus mūrum ostendit. ecce! Marcus hunc titulum 20
vīdit: "Marcus Āfrō favet. Āfer est candidātus optimus."

"euge! hic titulus mē valdē dēlectat," inquit Marcus.

Quārtus alterum titulum in mūrō cōnspcxit:

"Quārtus Holcōniō favet. Holcōnius est candidātus optimus."

Quārtus quoque laetissimus erat. 25

frātrēs Sullae trīgintā dēnāriōs dedērunt. Sulla rīdēbat. postquam Marcus et Quārtus discessērunt, tertium titulum addidit:

"Marcus et Quārtus sunt līberālissimī."

Words and Phrases

asinus	*ass, donkey*	dēsistite!	*stop!*
senior	*the older*	intrō īte!	*go inside!*
ērāde!	*erase!*	rem cōnfēcit	*finished the job*
īnscrīptiōnem	*writing*	tertium	*third*
ērāsit	*erased*	addidit	*added*
		līberālissimī	*very generous*

Lūcius Spurius Pompōniānus

in vīllā

Grumiō ē culīnā contendit. Clēmēns Grumiōnem videt.

Clēmēns: babae! togam splendidam geris!
Grumiō: placetne tibi?
Clēmēns: mihi placet. quō festīnās, Grumiō?
Grumiō: ad amphitheātrum contendō. Āfer fautōrēs exspectat.   5
Clēmēns: num tū Āfrō favēs? Caecilius Holcōniō favet.
Grumiō: Āfer fautōribus quīnque dēnāriōs prōmīsit. Holcōnius fautōribus duōs dēnāriōs tantum prōmīsit. ego Āfrō faveō, quod vir līberālis est.
Clēmēns: sed tū servus es. cīvis Pompēiānus nōn es. Āfer cīvibus   10 Pompēiānīs pecūniam prōmīsit.
Grumiō: Clēmēns, hodiē nōn sum Grumiō. hodiē sum Lūcius Spurius Pompōniānus!
Clēmēns: Lūcius Spurius Pompōniānus! mendācissimus coquus es!   15
Grumiō: minimē! hodiē sum pistor Pompēiānus. hodiē nōs pistōrēs ad amphitheātrum convenīmus. nōs Āfrum ad forum dūcimus, ubi cīvēs ōrātiōnēs exspectant. ego ad amphitheātrum contendō. tū mēcum venīs?
Clēmēns: tēcum veniō. Āfrō nōn faveō. dēnāriōs nōn cupiō, sed dē   20 tē sollicitus sum. rem perīculōsam suscipis.
(exeunt.)

Words and Phrases

babae!	*hey!*	convenīmus	*gather, meet*
quō?	*where?*	ōrātiōnēs	*speeches*
fautōrēs	*supporters*	mēcum	*with me*
quīnque	*five*	dē tē	*about you*
prōmīsit	*promised*	perīculōsam	*dangerous*
tantum	*only*	suscipis	*you are undertaking*
mendācissimus	*very deceitful*	exeunt	*they go out*

prope amphitheātrum

multī pistōrēs ad amphitheātrum conveniunt. Grumiō et Clēmēns ad hanc turbam festīnant.

dīvīsor: festīnāte! festīnāte! nōs Āfrum exspectāmus.

Grumiō: salvē, dīvīsor! ego sum Lūcius Spurius Pompōniānus et hic (*Grumiō Clēmentem pulsat*) servus meus est. ego et Āfer   5
amīcissimī sumus.

dīvīsor: ecce quīnque dēnāriī!
(dīvīsor Grumiōnī dēnāriōs dat. dīvīsor Grumiōnī fūstem quoque trādit.)

Grumiō: Āfer mihi dēnāriōs, nōn fūstem prōmīsit.   10

Clēmēns: Āfer vir līberālis est.

Grumiō: tacē, pessime serve!

dīvīsor: fūstēs ūtilissimī sunt. Holcōnius et amīcī sunt in forō.

pistor: ecce Āfer! Āfer adest!
(Āfer et fautōrēs per viās ad forum contendunt.)   15

Words and Phrases

dīvīsor	*distributor (hired to distribute bribes at elections)*	amīcissimī	*very friendly, very good friends*
		tacē!	*shut up! be quiet!*
festīnāte!	*hurry!*	ūtilissimī	*very useful*

in forō

pistōrēs cum Clēmente et cum Grumiōne Āfrum ad forum dūcunt.

pistor prīmus: Pompēiānī Āfrō favent.

pistor secundus: Āfer est melior quam Holcōnius.

pistor tertius: nōs Āfrō crēdimus.

Clēmēns: Grumiō! in forō sunt Holcōnius et amīcī.   5
Holcōnium et amīcōs videō.

Grumiō: euge! fēminās videō, ancillās videō, puellās
. . . ēheu! Caecilium videō! Caecilius cum Holcōniō stat! ad vīllam reveniō!

Clēmēns: Grumiō, manē!   10
(Grumiō fugit.)

mercātor prīmus: Holcōnius est vir nōbilis.

mercātor secundus: Holcōnius melior est quam Āfer.

mercātor tertius: nōs mercātōrēs Holcōniō favēmus.
(pistōrēs et mercātōrēs conveniunt. īrātī sunt.)   15

---

pistor prīmus:	Holcōnius est asinus. vōs quoque estis asinī, quod Holcōniō crēditis.
mercātor prīmus:	Āfer est caudex. vōs quoque estis caudicēs, quod Āfrō crēditis.
pistor secundus:	amīcī! mercātōrēs nōs "caudicēs" vocant. nōs 20 nōn sumus caudicēs. fortissimī sumus. fūstēs habēmus.
mercātor secundus:	amīcī! pistōrēs nōs "asinōs" vocant. nōs nōn sumus asinī. nōs fortiōrēs sumus quam pistōrēs. magnōs fūstēs habēmus. 25 *(mercātōrēs et pistōrēs in forō pugnant.)*

caudex   *blockhead, idiot*

in culīnā

Clēmēns in culīnā sedet. Grumiō intrat.

Clēmēns:	salvē, Pompōniāne! hercle! toga tua scissa est!
Grumiō:	ēheu! Holcōnius et amīcī in forō mē cēpērunt. postquam fūstem meum cōnspexērunt, clāmābant, "ecce pistor fortis!" tum mercātōrēs mē verberāvērunt. dēnāriōs 5 meōs rapuērunt. nunc nūllōs dēnāriōs habeō.
Clēmēns:	ego decem dēnāriōs habeō!
Grumiō:	decem dēnāriōs?
Clēmēns:	Caecilius mihi decem dēnāriōs dedit, quod servus fidēlis sum. postquam pistōrēs et mercātōrēs pugnam 10 commīsērunt, Caecilius mē cōnspexit. duo pistōrēs Caecilium verberābant. dominus noster auxilium postulābat. Caecilius mēcum ē forō effūgit. dominus noster mihi decem dēnāriōs dedit, quod līberālis est.
Grumiō:	Caecilius est . . . 15
Clēmēns:	valē, Pompōniāne!
Grumiō:	quō festīnās, Clēmēns?
Clēmēns:	ad portum festīnō. ibi Poppaea mē exspectat. placetne tibi?
Grumiō:	mihi nōn placet! 20

Words and Phrases

scissa	*torn*	auxilium	*help*
rapuērunt	*seized, grabbed*	effūgit	*escaped*

About the Language

1 In Stage 9, you met the dative case:

Quīntus **servō** pecūniam dedit.　*Quintus gave money **to the slave.***

2 In Stage 11, you have met some further examples:

mercātōrēs **agricolīs** respondent.　*The merchants reply **to the farmers.***

Quārtus **Holcōniō** favet.　*Quartus gives support **to Holconius.***

nōs **pistōrī** crēdimus.　*We have faith **in the baker.***

3 Some of the sentences above can be translated more simply:

Quārtus Holcōniō favet.　*Quartus supports Holconius.*

nōs pistōrī crēdimus.　*We trust the baker.*

4 Further examples:

1 nōs Āfrō favēmus.
2 vōs Holcōniō crēditis.
3 mercātōrēs candidātō nostrō nōn crēdunt.
4 pistōrēs mercātōribus respondent.

5 Notice the dative of **nōs** and **vōs**:

nōs sumus fortēs. deī **nōbīs** imperium dant.
We are brave. The gods give an empire to us.

vōs estis ignāvī. deī **vōbīs** nihil dant.
You are cowardly. The gods give nothing to you.

6 Notice the following use of the dative:

"placetne **tibi**?" "**mihi** placet."
"Is is pleasing to you?" "It is pleasing to me."

There are many other ways of translating these examples, such as:

"Does it please you?" "It pleases me."
"Is it all right for you?" "Yes, it is."

Practicing the Language

1 Complete each sentence with the right word from the list below, and then translate it. Do not use any word more than once.

contendō   faveō
contendis   favēs
contendimus   favēmus
contenditis   favētis

1 ego ad forum . . . . . . ego sum fautor.
2 tū Āfrō . . . . . . tū es caudex.
3 ego Holcōniō . . . . . ., quod Holcōnius est candidātus optimus.
4 nōs Holcōniō nōn . . . . . ., quod Holcōnius est asinus.
5 Clēmēns, cūr tū ad portum . . . . . ?
6 vōs Āfrō . . . . . ., quod vōs estis pistōrēs.
7 nōs ad vīllam . . . . . ., quod in forō sunt Holcōnius et amīcī.
8 ēheu! cūr ē forō . . . . . . ? vōs dēnāriōs meōs habētis!

2 Complete each sentence with the right word, and then translate it.

1 Quārtus Sullae decem dēnāriōs dedit. Sulla . . . . . . in mūrō scrīpsit. (titulus, titulum)
2 fūr vīllam intrābat. subitō . . . . . . lātrāvit. (canis, canem)
3 multī candidātī sunt in forō. ego . . . . . . videō. (Holcōnius, Holcōnium)
4 ego ad portum currō. . . . . . . mē exspectat. (ancilla, ancillae)
5 hodiē ad urbem contendō. in amphitheātrō sunt . . . . (gladiātor, gladiātōrēs)
6 rhētor est īrātus. rhētor . . . . . . exspectat. (puerī, puerōs)
7 fēminae sunt in tabernā. mercātōrēs fēminīs . . . . . . ostendunt. (stolae, stolās)
8 postquam Holcōnius et amīcī Grumiōnem cēpērunt, quīnque . . . . . . rapuērunt. (dēnāriī, dēnāriōs)

About the Language

1 So far you have met the following ways of asking questions in Latin:

   1 (From Stage 4 onwards) By means of a question-word such as **quis? quid? ubi? cūr?**

quis est Quīntus?	*Who is Quīntus?*
quid tū facis?	*What are you doing?*
ubi est ānulus?	*Where is the ring?*
cūr lacrimās?	*Why are you crying?*

   2 (From Stage 4 onwards) By tone of voice, indicated in writing by means of a question-mark:

tū pecūniam dēbēs?	*Do you owe the money?*
tū ānulum habēs?	*Do you have the ring?*

   3 (From Stage 10 onwards) By adding **-ne** to the first word of the sentence:

vōsne estis contentī?	*Are you satisfied?*
placetne tibi?	*Does it please you?*

   4 (From Stage 7 onwards) By means of the question-word **num?** This word is used to suggest that the answer to the question will be *no*. Notice the different ways of translating it:

num tū timēs?	*Surely you're not afraid?*
	You're not afraid, are you?
num vīnum bibis?	*Surely you're not drinking wine?*
	You're not drinking wine, are you?

2 Further examples:

   1 cūr tū in hortō labōrās?
   2 quis est āthlēta ille?
   3 tū discum habēs?
   4 vōsne estis īrātī?
   5 ubi sunt mercātōrēs?
   6 quid quaeris, domina?
   7 tūne Pompēiānus es?
   8 quis vīnum portat?
   9 cēnam parās?
  10 num cēnam parās?

Local Government and Elections

Pompeii, like other Roman towns, was responsible for managing its own local government. Every year, two pairs of officials were elected by the people. The senior pair, called **duovirī**, were responsible for hearing evidence and giving judgment in court. The other pair, called **aedīlēs**, had the task of supervising the public markets, the police force, the baths, places of public entertainment, the water supply and sewers. It was their duty to see that the public services were efficiently run and the local taxes spent wisely.

In addition to these four officials, there was a town governing board of one hundred leading citizens, most of whom had already served as duoviri or aediles. New members were chosen not by the people but by the town board itself.

The Pompeians took local politics seriously and the annual elections, which were held at the end of March, were very lively. As soon as the names of candidates were published, election fever gripped the town. Slogans appeared on the walls, groups of **fautōrēs** (*supporters*) held processions through the streets, and the candidates spoke at public meetings in the forum.

The town of Pompeii, with Vesuvius in the background

Many of the thousands of wall slogans found in Pompeii refer to the elections held there in March A.D. 79. Here are two of them:

"Casellius for aedile."

"We want Titus Claudius Verus for duovir."

It appears that these slogans were often painted on the walls at night by torchlight, either because the streets were then more or less deserted and so there was less risk of trouble from rival supporters, or because it was easier at night to put up a ladder for an hour or two without causing congestion on the sidewalks.

Political supporters represented all kinds of people and interests. Sometimes they were groups of neighbors, **vīcīnī**, who lived in the same area as the candidate. They would certainly include the candidate's personal friends and his clientes. Often, however, a candidate was nominated and supported by a particular trade group. One slogan reads:

"The barbers recommend Trebius for aedile."

Another says:

"Innkeepers, vote for Sallustius Capito!"

Mule-drivers, pack-carriers, bakers, fishermen: all expressed their support for their chosen candidate.

This method of electioneering by wall slogans naturally invited replies by rival supporters. One candidate, Vatia, was made to look ridiculous by this comment:

"All the people who are fast asleep vote for Vatia."

Pompeian women did not have the right to vote. Only adult male citizens were allowed to cast votes in the voting hall on election day. Nevertheless, women certainly took a lively interest in local politics and supported the various candidates vigorously. They painted slogans and marched through the streets carrying signs.

The candidates themselves wore a specially whitened toga in order to be easily recognized. The word **candidātus** is connected with **candidus**, which means *dazzling white*. As they walked around greeting voters, they were accompanied by agents, who praised their qualities, made promises on their behalf, and distributed bribes in the form of money. This financial bribery was illegal but was widely practiced. Legal forms of persuasion included promises of games and entertainments if the candidate won. In fact, it was expected that those who were elected would show their gratitude to the voters by putting on splendid shows in the theater and amphitheater at their own expense.

A successful candidate would also be expected to contribute from his own wealth to the construction or repair of public buildings. We know that the temple of Fortuna Augusta, situated just to the north of the forum, was built largely by the generosity of Marcus Tullius who owned the whole of the site on which it was built. The family of the Holconii, whose names often appear in the lists of Pompeian duoviri and aediles, were connected with the building of the large theater, and another wealthy family, the Flacci, helped to pay for the other civic buildings. The Flacci also had a reputation for putting on first class entertainments.

This tradition of public service was encouraged by the emperors, and was an important part of Roman public life. It made it possible for a small town like Pompeii to enjoy benefits which could not have been paid for by local taxes alone. It also meant that men who wanted to take part in the government of their town had to be wealthy. The number of families in Pompeii who could afford to hold office regularly was about fifty.

Although public service was unpaid and was not a means of making money, it gave a man a position of importance in his town. The wide seats in the front row of the theater, which gave a close-up view of the chorus and actors, were reserved for him; he also had a special place close to the arena in the amphitheater. In due course, the town governing board might erect a statue to him, and he would have his name inscribed on any building to whose construction or repair he had contributed. The Romans were not particularly modest people. They were eager for honor and fame among their fellow citizens. There was therefore no shortage of candidates to compete for these rewards at election time.

We said at the beginning of this account of local government that Pompeii was free to run its own affairs. But if the local officials were unable to preserve law and order, the central government at Rome might take over and run the town. This actually happened after the famous riot in A.D. 59 described in Stage 8, when the people of nearby Nuceria quarreled with the Pompeians at a gladiatorial show given by Livineus Regulus, and many were killed or wounded. The Nucerians complained to the Emperor Nero; Regulus himself was sent into exile and games in Pompeii were banned for ten years. In the following year, A.D. 60, Nero dismissed the duoviri and appointed a special officer or **praefectus** to run the affairs of the town. This was a strong sign of official disapproval and two years passed before the local people were again trusted to take care of themselves.

Words and Phrases Checklist

convenit	*gathers, meets*
crēdit	*trusts, believes, has faith in*
dē	*down from; about*
favet	*favors, supports*
gēns	*family*
invītat	*invites*
legit	*reads*
līberālis	*generous*
minimē!	*no!*
mūrus	*wall*
noster	*our*
nunc	*now*
placet	*it pleases, suits*
prīmus	*first*
prōmittit	*promises*
pugna	*fight*
rapit	*seizes, grabs*
secundus	*second*
senātor	*senator*
sollicitus	*worried, anxious*
stultus	*stupid*
tertius	*third*
ūtilis	*useful*
valē!	*good-by!*
verberat	*strikes, beats*
vir	*man*

Word Search

Match each definition with one of the words given below.

incredible, liberal, mural, placate, solicitude, stultify, utilitarian

1 . . . . . : a wall-painting or -drawing
2 . . . . . : to cause to appear foolish
3 . . . . . : practical, functional
4 . . . . . : to soothe or pacify
5 . . . . . : anxious concern
6 . . . . . : unbelievable
7 . . . . . : generous; free-thinking

Stage 12

mōns Vesuvius

Syphāx et Celer in portū
stābant.
amīcī montem spectābant.

Syphāx amīcō dīxit,
"ego prope portum servōs
vēndēbam. ego subitō
sonōs audīvī."

Celer Syphācī respondit,
"tū sonōs audīvistī. ego
tremōrēs sēnsī. ego prope
montem ambulābam."

Poppaea et Lucriō in ātriō
stābant. sollicitī erant.

Poppaea Lucriōnī dīxit,
"ego in forō eram. ego tibi
togam quaerēbam. ego
nūbem mīrābilem cōnspexī."

Lucriō Poppaeae respondit,
"tū nūbem cōnspexistī. ego
cinerem sēnsī. ego flammās
vīdī."

Marcus et Quārtus in forō erant.
Sulla ad frātrēs contendit.

Sulla frātribus dīxit,
"ego ad theātrum contendēbam.
ego sonōs audīvī et tremōrēs
sēnsī. vōs sonōs audīvistis?
vōs tremōrēs sēnsistis?"

frātrēs Sullae respondērunt,
"nōs tremōrēs sēnsimus
et sonōs audīvimus.
nōs nūbem mīrābilem vīdimus.
nōs sollicitī sumus."

When you have read this story, answer the questions at the end.

tremōrēs

Caecilius cum Iūliō cēnābat. Iūlius in vīllā splendidā prope Nūceriam habitābat.

Iūlius Caeciliō dīxit, "ego sollicitus sum. ego in hortō heri ambulābam et librum legēbam. subitō terra valdē tremuit. ego tremōrēs sēnsī. quid tū agēbās?" 5

"ego servō epistulās dictābam," inquit Caecilius. "ego quoque tremōrēs sēnsī. postquam terra tremuit, Grumiō tablīnum intrāvit et mē ad hortum dūxit. nōs nūbem mīrābilem vīdimus."

"vōs timēbātis?" rogāvit Iūlius.

"nōs nōn timēbāmus," Caecilius Iūliō respondit. "ego, postquam 10 nūbem cōnspexī, familiam meam ad larārium vocāvī. tum nōs laribus sacrificium fēcimus."

"vōs fortissimī erātis," clāmāvit Iūlius. "vōs tremōrēs sēnsistis, vōs nūbem cōnspexistis. vōs tamen nōn erātis perterritī."

"nōs nōn timēbāmus, quod nōs laribus crēdēbāmus," inquit 15 Caecilius. "iamprīdem terra tremuit. iamprīdem tremōrēs vīllās et mūrōs dēlēvērunt. sed larēs vīllam meam et familiam meam servāvērunt. ego igitur sollicitus nōn sum."

subitō servus triclīnium intrāvit.

"domine, Clēmēns est in ātriō. Clēmēns ex urbe vēnit. Caecilium 20 quaerit," servus Iūliō dīxit.

"nōn intellegō," Caecilius exclāmāvit. "ego Clēmentem ad fundum meum māne mīsī."

Words and Phrases

tremōrēs	*tremors*	familiam	*household*
tremuit	*shook*	larārium	*domestic shrine*
sēnsī	*felt*	laribus	*household gods*
agēbās	*were doing*	sacrificium	*sacrifice*
epistulās	*letters*	iamprīdem	*a long time ago*
dictābam	*was dictating*	fundum	*farm*
nūbem	*cloud*		

Names and Proper Adjectives

cum Iūliō *with Julius*

servus Clēmentem in triclīnium dūxit.

"cūr tū ē fundō discessistī? cūr tū ad hanc vīllam vēnistī?" rogāvit   25
Caecilius.

Clēmēns dominō et Iūliō rem tōtam nārrāvit.

Questions

1 Why was Julius worried?
2 What had Caecilius been doing when the tremors began?
3 What did Caecilius and Grumio see when they went into the garden?
4 What did Caecilius do then?
5 Why was Caecilius so sure that his household gods would protect him?
6 What news did Julius' slave bring?
7 Why did this news puzzle Caecilius?

ad urbem

"ego ad fundum tuum contendī," Clēmēns dominō dīxit. "ego vīlicō epistulam tuam trādidī. postquam vīlicus epistulam lēgit, nōs fundum et servōs īnspiciēbāmus. subitō nōs ingentēs sonōs audīvimus. nōs tremōrēs quoque sēnsimus. tum ego montem spectāvī et nūbem mīrābilem vīdī."   5

"quid vōs fēcistis?" rogāvit Iūlius.

"nōs urbem petīvimus, quod valdē timēbāmus," respondit Clēmēns. "ego, postquam urbem intrāvī, clāmōrem ingentem audīvī. multī Pompēiānī per viās currēbant. fēminae cum īnfantibus per urbem festīnābant. fīliī et fīliae parentēs quaerēbant. ego ad   10
vīllam nostram pervēnī, ubi Metella et Quīntus manēbant. Quīntus mē ad tē mīsit, quod nōs omnēs perterritī erāmus."

Caecilius ad urbem contendit, quod sollicitus erat. Iūlius et Clēmēns quoque ad urbem festīnāvērunt. maxima turba viās complēbat, quod Pompēiānī ē vīllīs festīnābant.   15

prope urbem Holcōnium cōnspexērunt. Holcōnius cum servīs ad portum fugiēbat.

"cūr vōs ad urbem contenditis? cūr nōn ad portum fugitis?" rogāvit Holcōnius.

"ad vīllam meam contendō," Caecilius Holcōniō respondit. 20
"Metellam et Quīntum quaerō. tū Metellam vīdistī? Quīntum
cōnspexistī?"

"ēheu!" clāmāvit Holcōnius. "ego vīllam splendidam habēbam.
in vīllā erant statuae pulchrae et pictūrae pretiōsae. iste mōns
vīllam meam dēlēvit; omnēs statuae sunt frāctae." 25

"sed, amīce, tū uxōrem meam vīdistī?" rogāvit Caecilius.

"ego nihil dē Metellā scio. nihil cūrō," respondit Holcōnius.

"furcifer!" clāmāvit Caecilius. "tū vīllam tuam āmīsistī. ego
uxōrem meam āmīsī!"

Caecilius, postquam Holcōnium vituperāvit, ad urbem 30
contendit.

Words and Phrases

vīlicō	*overseer, manager*	pervēnī	*reached, arrived at*
sonōs	*noises*	iste mōns	*that mountain*
fīliae	*daughters*	scio	*know*
parentēs	*parents*	nihil cūrō	*I don't care*

ad vīllam

in urbe pavor maximus erat. cinis iam dēnsior incidēbat. flammae ubīque erant. Caecilius et amīcī, postquam urbem intrāvērunt, vīllam petēbant. sed iter erat difficile, quod multī Pompēiānī viās complēbant. Caecilius tamen per viās fortiter contendēbat.

nūbēs iam dēnsissima erat. subitō Iūlius exclāmāvit, 5
"vōs ad vīllam contendite! ego nōn valeō."

statim ad terram dēcidit exanimātus. Clēmēns Iūlium ad templum proximum portāvit.

"tū optimē fēcistī," Caecilius servō dīxit. "tū Iūlium servāvistī. ego tibi lībertātem prōmittō." 10

tum Caecilius ē templō discessit et ad vīllam cucurrit.

Clēmēns cum Iūliō in templō manēbat. tandem Iūlius respīrāvit. "ubi sumus?" rogāvit.

"sumus tūtī," servus Iūliō respondit. "dea Īsis nōs servāvit. postquam tū in terram dēcidistī, ego tē ad hoc templum portāvī." 15

"tibi grātiās maximās agō, quod tū mē servāvistī," inquit Iūlius. "sed ubi est Caecilius?"

"dominus meus ad vīllam contendit," respondit Clēmēns.

"ēheu! stultissimus est Caecilius!" clāmāvit Iūlius. "sine dubiō Metella et Quīntus mortuī sunt. ego ex urbe quam celerrimē 20 discēdō. tū mēcum venīs?"

"minimē, amīce!" Clēmēns Iūliō respondit. "ego dominum meum quaerō!"

Words and Phrases

pavor	*panic*	exanimātus	*unconscious*
cinis	*ash*	templum	*temple*
iam	*now*	proximum	*nearest*
dēnsior	*thicker*	lībertātem	*freedom*
incidēbat	*was falling*	respīrāvit	*recovered consciousness, revived*
flammae	*flames*	tūtī	*safe*
iter	*journey, progress*	dea	*goddess*
difficile	*difficult*	sine dubiō	*without a doubt*
valeō	*I feel well*		

Names and Proper Adjectives

Īsis   *Isis (Great Mother goddess of Egypt)*

Vesuvius in eruption, 1817: watercolor by J.M.W. Turner

fīnis

iam nūbēs ātra ad terram dēscendēbat; iam cinis dēnsissimus incidēbat. plūrimī Pompēiānī iam dē urbe suā dēspērābant. multī in flammīs perībant. Clēmēns tamen nōn dēspērābat, sed obstinātē vīllam petīvit, quod Caecilium quaerēbat. tandem ad vīllam pervēnit. sollicitus ruīnās spectāvit. tōta vīlla ardēbat. Clēmēns   5
fūmum ubīque vīdit. per ruīnās tamen fortiter contendit et dominum suum vocāvit. Caecilius tamen nōn respondit. subitō canis lātrāvit. servus tablīnum intrāvit, ubi canis erat. Cerberus dominum custōdiēbat.

Caecilius in tablīnō moribundus iacēbat. mūrus sēmirutus eum   10
paene cēlābat. Clēmēns dominō vīnum dedit. Caecilius, postquam vīnum bibit, sēnsim respīrāvit.

"quid accidit, domine?" rogāvit Clēmēns.

"ego ad vīllam vēnī," inquit Caecilius. "Metellam nōn vīdī! Quīntum nōn vīdī! vīlla erat dēserta. tum ego ad tablīnum   15
contendēbam. subitō terra tremuit et pariēs in mē incidit. tū es servus fidēlis. abī! ego tē iubeō. dē vītā meā dēspērō. Metella et Quīntus periērunt. nunc ego quoque sum moritūrus."

Clēmēns recūsāvit. in tablīnō obstinātē manēbat. Caecilius iterum clāmāvit: 20

"Clēmēns, abī! tē iubeō. fortasse Quīntus superfuit. quaere Quīntum! hunc ānulum Quīntō dā!"

Caecilius, postquam Clēmentī ānulum suum trādidit, statim exspīrāvit. Clēmēns dominō trīste valedīxit et ē vīllā discessit.

Cerberus tamen in vīllā mānsit. dominum frūstrā custōdiēbat.   25

Words and Phrases

fīnis	end	sēnsim	slowly, gradually
ātra	black	accidit	happened
dēscendēbat	was coming down	pariēs	wall
plūrimī	most	iubeō	order
perībant	were dying, were perishing	moritūrus	going to die
obstinātē	stubbornly	recūsāvit	refused
ruīnās	ruins, wreckage	superfuit	has survived
fūmum	smoke	exspīrāvit	died
moribundus	almost dead	trīste	sadly
sēmirutus	half-collapsed	valedīxit	said good-by

About the Language

1 In Stage 6 you met the imperfect and perfect tenses:

IMPERFECT	PERFECT
portābat	portāvit
he was carrying	*he carried*
portābant	portāvērunt
they were carrying	*they carried*

2 In Stage 12 you have met the imperfect and perfect tenses in sentences with *I*, *you*, and *we*:

IMPERFECT	PERFECT
(ego) portābam	(ego) portāvī
I was carrying	*I carried*
(tū) portābās	(tū) portāvistī
you (singular) were carrying	*you (singular) carried*
(nōs) portābāmus	(nōs) portāvimus
we were carrying	*we carried*
(vōs) portābātis	(vōs) portāvistis
you (plural) were carrying	*you (plural) carried*

ego, tū, nōs, and **vōs** are usually left out.

3 The words for *was* and *were* are as follows:

(ego)	eram	*I was*
(tū)	erās	*you (singular) were*
	erat	*s/he, it was*
(nōs)	erāmus	*we were*
(vōs)	erātis	*you (plural) were*
	erant	*they were*

Skeletons found at Herculaneum

The Destruction and Excavation of Pompeii

On the night of 23–24 August A.D.79, it rained hard; a strong wind blew and earth tremors were felt. During the following morning, Vesuvius, which had been an inactive volcano for many centuries, erupted with enormous violence. A huge mass of mud poured down the mountainside and swallowed the town of Herculaneum; hot stones and ash descended in vast quantities on Pompeii, burying everything to a depth of fifteen to twenty feet (four-and-a-half to six meters). Most people, with vivid memories of the earthquake seventeen years before, fled into the open countryside carrying a few possessions, but others remained behind, hoping that the storm would pass. They died, buried in the ruins of their homes or suffocated by sulfur fumes.

The next day, the whole area was a desert of white ash. Here and there the tops of buildings could be seen, and little groups of survivors struggled back to salvage what they could. They dug tunnels to get down to their homes and rescue furniture, valuables, and paintings. But nothing could be done to excavate and rebuild the town itself. The site

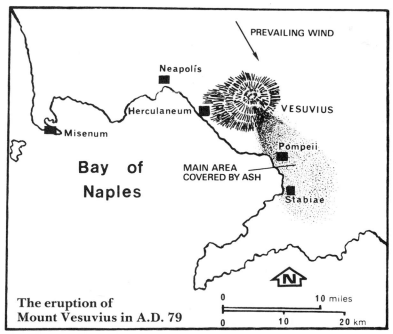

The eruption of
Mount Vesuvius in A.D. 79

The eruption of Mount Vesuvius in March 1944

was abandoned; thousands of refugees made new homes in Naples and other Campanian towns. Gradually the ruins collapsed, a new layer of soil covered the site, and Pompeii disappeared from view.

During the Middle Ages, nobody knew exactly where the town lay. Only a vague memory survived in the name "cività" by which the local people still called the low hill. But what city it was or whether there really was a city buried there, they did not know and certainly did not care.

The first remains were found in 1594 when an Italian architect called Fontana was constructing a water channel from the River Sarno to a nearby town. He discovered the remains of buildings and an inscription. But these were misunderstood, as it was thought that a villa belonging to the famous Roman politician, Pompeius, had been discovered. Nothing much was done for another 150 years, until in 1748, Charles III, King of Naples, began to excavate the site in search of treasure. In 1763, the treasure seekers realized they were exploring the lost city of Pompeii. At Herculaneum the excavations were much more difficult because the volcanic mud had turned to hard rock and the town lay up to forty feet (twelve meters) below the new ground level. Tunneling down was slow and dangerous work.

In the early days of excavation, no effort was made to uncover the sites in an orderly way; the methods of modern archaeology were unknown.

The excavators were not interested in uncovering towns in order to learn about the people who lived there, but were looking for jewelry, pictures, bronze statues, and other works of art, which were then taken away to decorate the palaces of kings and rich men.

At the beginning of the nineteenth century, however, the looting was stopped and systematic excavation began. Section by section, the soil and rubble were cleared. The most fragile and precious objects were taken to the National Museum of Naples, but everything else was kept where it was found. As buildings were uncovered, they were partly reconstructed with original materials to preserve them and make them safe for visitors.

From time to time, archaeologists still find a hollow space in the ash where an object of wood or other organic material has perished. To find out what it was, they pour liquid plaster into the hole, and when it has hardened they carefully remove the surrounding ash, and are left with a perfect image of the original object. In this way, many wooden doors and shutters have been discovered, and also bodies of human beings and animals.

The work is not yet finished. Only about three-fifths of Pompeii has so far been uncovered and less of Herculaneum. Whenever a new house is opened up, the archaeologist finds it just as it was abandoned. He may discover the remains of a meal, pots on the stove, coins in the tablinum, lampstands in various rooms, paintings (often only slightly damaged) on the walls, the lead pipes which supplied water to the fountains in the garden, brooches, needles, jars of cosmetics, shoes, and writing-tablets; in fact all the hundreds of small things that went to make up a Roman home. If he is lucky, he may also discover the name of the family that lived there.

Thus, through the efforts of the archaeologist, a remarkably detailed picture of the life of this ordinary Roman town has emerged from the disaster which destroyed it 2,000 years ago.

Words and Phrases Checklist

āmittit	*loses*	igitur	*therefore*
cinis	*ash*	incidit	*falls*
complet	*fills*	mīrābilis	*marvelous, strange, wonderful*
custōdit	*guards*	mittit	*sends*
dēnsus	*thick*	mōns	*mountain*
epistula	*letter*	nūbēs	*cloud*
flamma	*flame*	optimē	*very well*
fortiter	*bravely*	paene	*nearly, almost*
frūstrā	*in vain*	sentit	*feels*
fugit	*runs away, flees*	tandem	*at last*
fundus	*farm*	templum	*temple*
iacet	*lies*	terra	*ground, land*
iam	*now*	timet	*is afraid, fears*

You have also met the following numbers:

ūnus	*one*
duo	*two*
trēs	*three*

Word Search

Match each definition with one of the words given below.

complete, custodian, density, frustrate, fugitive, incident, incinerate

1 . . . . . : finished
2 . . . . . : a runaway
3 . . . . . : to thwart or disappoint
4 . . . . . : a caretaker
5 . . . . . : thickness
6 . . . . . : an event
7 . . . . . : to burn

Language
Information
Section

PART ONE: Review Grammar

Nouns

1 Words like **puella, servus, mercātor,** and **leō,** which change their endings to form a nominative case, accusative case, etc., are known as *nouns*. They often indicate people (or animals), e.g. **amīcus** and **canis;** they can also indicate places (e.g. **taberna, hortus**) or things (e.g. **discus, statua**).

2 In Unit 1, you have learned three of the five most common cases:

	first declension	*second declension*	*third declension*	
SINGULAR				
nominative	**puella**	**servus**	**mercātor**	**leō**
genitive (not yet learned)				
dative	**puellae**	**servō**	**mercātōrī**	**leōnī**
accusative	**puellam**	**servum**	**mercātōrem**	**leōnem**
ablative (not yet learned)				
PLURAL				
nominative	**puellae**	**servī**	**mercātōrēs**	**leōnēs**
genitive (not yet learned)				
dative	**puellīs**	**servīs**	**mercātōribus**	**leōnibus**
accusative	**puellās**	**servōs**	**mercātōrēs**	**leōnēs**
ablative (not yet learned)				

3 Review the way the cases are used:

nominative: **mercātor** cantābat. *The merchant was singing.*
servī labōrābant. *The slaves were working.*

dative: senex **mercātōrī** pictūram ostendit.
The old man showed the painting to the merchant.

lībertī **puellīs** vīnum trādidērunt.
The freedmen handed over the wine to the girls.

accusative: Grumiō **puellam** salūtāvit.
Grumio greeted the girl.

Caecilius **servōs** vituperāvit.
Caecilius cursed the slaves.

4 Translate each sentence, then change the word in boldface from the singular to the plural, and translate again.

For example: puerī **servum** vīdērunt.   *The boys saw the slave.*
This becomes: puerī **servōs** vīdērunt.   *The boys saw the slaves.*

1 puerī **leōnem** vīdērunt.
2 dominus **puellam** audīvit.
3 centuriō **amīcum** salūtāvit.
4 agricolae **gladiātōrem** laudāvērunt.
5 cīvēs **servō** pecūniam trādidērunt.
6 coquus **mercātōrī** cēnam parāvit.

5 Translate each sentence, then change the word in boldface from the plural to the singular, and translate again.

For example: vēnāliciī **mercātōribus** pecūniam dedērunt.
The slave-dealers gave money to the merchants.

This becomes: vēnāliciī **mercātōrī** pecūniam dedērunt.
The slave-dealers gave money to the merchant.

1 dominus **servōs** īnspexit.
2 āthlētae **mercātōrēs** vituperāvērunt.
3 vēnālicius **ancillās** vēndēbat.
4 senex **āctōrēs** spectābat.
5 gladiātōrēs **leōnibus** cibum dedērunt.
6 iuvenēs **puellīs** statuam ostendērunt.

Verbs

1 Words like **portō** (*I carry*), **doceō** (*I teach*), **trahō** (*I drag*), **capiō** (*I take*), and **audiō** (*I hear*), which change their endings in the way shown below, are known as *verbs*. They usually indicate an action, e.g. **currō** (*I run*), **necāvit** (*he killed*), or a state of affairs, e.g. **dormiēbant** (*they were asleep*).

2 In Unit 1, you have learned the following forms of the verb:

first conjugation		*second conjugation*	*third conjugation*	*third con-jugation "-iō"*	*fourth conjugation*
PRESENT TENSE					
I carry	**portō**	**doceō**	**trahō**	**capiō**	**audiō**
you (sg.) carry	**portās**	**docēs**	**trahis**	**capis**	**audīs**
s/he, it carries	**portat**	**docet**	**trahit**	**capit**	**audit**
we carry	**portāmus**	**docēmus**	**trahimus**	**capimus**	**audīmus**
you (pl.) carry	**portātis**	**docētis**	**trahitis**	**capitis**	**audītis**
they carry	**portant**	**docent**	**trahunt**	**capiunt** ·	**audiunt**
IMPERFECT TENSE					
s/he, it was carrying	**portābat**	**docēbat**	**trahēbat**	**capiēbat**	**audiēbat**
they were carrying	**portābant**	**docēbant**	**trahēbant**	**capiēbant**	**audiēbant**
PERFECT TENSE					
s/he, it carried	**portāvit**	**docuit**	**trāxit**	**cēpit**	**audīvit**
they carried	**portāvērunt**	**docuērunt**	**trāxērunt**	**cēpērunt**	**audīvērunt**

The other endings of the imperfect and perfect tenses are given on page 195.

3 **portō** belongs to a group of verbs known as the *first conjugation*. Other verbs in this group are **ambulō** and **labōrō**.

doceō belongs to a group of verbs known as the *second conjugation*. Also in this group are **sedeō** and **videō**.

trahō and **capiō** belong to a group of verbs known as the *third conjugation* (**capiō** belongs to a subgroup known as third conjugation "-iō" verbs). Also in this group and subgroup are **dīcō** and **faciō**.

audiō belongs to a group of verbs known as the *fourth conjugation*. Also in this group are **dormiō** and **veniō**.

Each of the four conjugations has a slightly different way of changing its endings.

4 In paragraph 2 opposite, find the Latin words for:

    1 They were carrying; they were teaching; she was dragging.
    2 He heard; they dragged; she taught; it took.
    3 I teach; we take; she hears; you (pl.) drag.

5 Translate these examples of the present tense:
    1 ego dormiō; servus dormit; nōs dormīmus; servī dormiunt.
    2 servī labōrant; tū labōrās; servus labōrat; ego labōrō.
    3 intrant; intrās; intrat; intrō.
    4 sedēmus; sedeō; sedent; sedēs.
    5 capiō; capimus; capiunt; capitis.
    6 veniō; venīmus; veniunt; venītis.

6 Further examples of all three tenses:

    1 servī ambulant; servī ambulābant; servī ambulāvērunt.
    2 servus labōrat; servus labōrābat; servus labōrāvit.
    3 clāmat; clāmābat; clāmāvit.
    4 dormit; dormiēbat; dormīvit.
    5 parābat; parāvit; parat.
    6 intrābant; intrāvērunt; intrant.
    7 fēcit; faciēbat; facit.
    8 dīxērunt; dīcunt; dīcēbant.
    9 appārēbant; appārent; appāruērunt.

7 English has more than one way of translating each of these tenses. In the present tense, for example, **portat** can mean either *s/he carries* or *s/he is carrying*. In the imperfect tense, **portābat** can mean either *s/he was carrying* or *s/he used to carry* or sometimes *s/he began to carry*. In the perfect tense, **parāvit** can mean *s/he prepared* or *s/he has prepared*.

8 A few verbs which do not belong to any of the four conjugations are known as *irregular* verbs. This is the most important one:

PRESENT TENSE		IMPERFECT TENSE	
sum	*I am*	**eram**	*I was*
es	*you (sg.) are*	**erās**	*you (sg.) were*
est	*s/he, it is*	**erat**	*s/he, it was*
sumus	*we are*	**erāmus**	*we were*
estis	*you (pl.) are*	**erātis**	*you (pl.) were*
sunt	*they are*	**erant**	*they were*

Ways of Forming the Perfect Tense

1 Notice the way in which most verbs in the first conjugation (e.g. **portat**, **salūtat**) form their perfect tense:

PRESENT

portat
s/he, it carries

portant
they carry

PERFECT

portāvit
s/he, it carried (or *has carried*)

portāvērunt
they carried (or *have carried*)

Further examples for study and translation:

salūtant
ambulat

salūtāvērunt
ambulāvit

2 Most verbs in the second conjugation (e.g. **docet, terret**) form their perfect tense like this:

docet
s/he, it teaches

terrent
they frighten

docuit
s/he, it taught (or *has taught*)

terruērunt
they frightened (or *have frightened*)

Further examples:

terret
appārent

terruit
appāruērunt

3 Third conjugation verbs (e.g. **dīcit, facit**) form their perfect tense in various ways. Consult the "Complete Vocabulary" for the perfect-tense form that is appropriate for each verb. Here are some examples:

trahit
s/he, it drags

trāxit
s/he, it dragged (or *has dragged*)

capit
s/he, it takes

cēpit
s/he, it took (or *has taken*)

Further examples for study and translation:

mittit	mīsit
dīcit	dīxit
dīcunt	dīxērunt
faciunt	fēcērunt

4 Most fourth conjugation verbs (e.g. **audit, dormit**) form their perfect tense like this:

audit
s/he, it hears

audīvit
s/he, it heard (or *has heard*)

Further examples:

dormit	dormīvit
dormiunt	dormīvērunt

5 Some verbs have unpredictable perfect-tense forms. Some examples from Unit 1 are:

manet
s/he, it remains

mānsit
s/he, it remained (or *has remained*)

discēdit
s/he, it leaves

discessit
s/he, it left (or *has left*)

manet and **discēdit** belong to different conjugations, but their perfect-tense forms have similar endings.

currit
s/he, it runs

cucurrit
s/he, it ran (or *has run*)

currit has a perfect-tense form with another syllable *on the front*.

videt
s/he, it sees

vīdit
s/he, it saw (or *has seen*)

videt has a perfect-tense form that is spelled *nearly* like it.

ostendit
s/he, it shows

ostendit
s/he, it showed (or *has shown*)

ostendit has a perfect-tense form that is spelled and pronounced *exactly* like it. Something similar can happen in English. For example, the words *yesterday* and *tomorrow* fix the tense of *hit* in the following English sentences:

Yesterday I hit a homer.   *Tomorrow I'll hit three homers.*

emit
s/he, it buys

ēmit
s/he, it bought (or *has bought*)

venit
s/he, it comes

vēnit
s/he, it came (or *has come*)

The Latin words for *bought* or *came* are spelled the same as the Latin words for *buys* or *comes*, but they are *pronounced* differently. The long mark over **ēmit** or **vēnit** is the sign for the different pronunciation. Something similar can happen in English, but if English is our native language, we do not need a special mark to help us remember that we should pronounce differently. Notice the two different pronunciations of *read* in the following English sentences:

"What's tomorrow's homework?"
"Read the story on page 6."
"Are you sure?"
"Yes, I read it on the blackboard before I left."

Word Order

1 The following word order is very common in Latin:

Milō discum īnspexit.   *Milo looked at the discus.*
mercātor togam vēndidit.   *The merchant sold the toga.*

2 From Stage 7 on, you have learned a slightly different example of the above word order:

discum īnspexit.   *He looked at the discus.*
togam vēndidit.   *He sold the toga.*
amīcum salūtāvit.   *She greeted the friend.*
theātrum intrāvērunt.   *They entered the theater.*

3 The following sentences are similar to those in paragraphs 1 and 2:

1 spectātōrēs Milōnem laudāvērunt.
2 Milōnem laudāvērunt.
3 senex agricolam cōnspexit.
4 statuam fēcit.
5 canēs et servī leōnem necāvērunt.
6 mercātor poētam et vēnālīcium vīdit.
7 poētam vīdit.
8 āthlētam salūtāvit.
9 mē salūtāvit.
10 tē salūtāvērunt.
11 Metella clāmōrem audīvit.
12 clāmōrem audīvit.

4 Remember that such words as **audīvit** can be translated not only as *he heard* but also as *she heard* or *it heard*.

5 Further examples:

1 Caecilius amīcum salūtat.
2 amīcum salūtat.
3 amīcum salūtās.
4 leōnem videō.
5 mē salūtās.
6 tē vituperō.

6 From Stage 9 on, you have learned to read longer sentences, involving the dative. The following word order is common in Latin:

vēnālīcius mercātōrī ancillam ostendit.
The slave-dealer showed the slave-girl to the merchant.

Further examples:

1 iuvenis Milōnī discum trādidit.
2 Metella fīliō dōnum ēmit.
3 dominus ancillīs signum dedit.
4 nūntiī cīvibus spectāculum nūntiāvērunt.
5 Quīntus mercātōrī et amīcīs togam ostendit.

Longer Sentences with "postquam" and "quod"

1 Compare these two sentences:

Pompēiānī gladiātōrēs vīdērunt.
The Pompeians saw the gladiators.

Pompēiānī, postquam amphitheātrum intrāvērunt, gladiātōrēs vīdērunt.
The Pompeians, after they entered the amphitheater, saw the gladiators.
        Or, in more natural English:
After the Pompeians entered the amphitheater, they saw the gladiators.

2 The next example is similar:

servī umbram timēbant.
The slaves were afraid of the ghost.

servī, quod erant ignāvī, umbram timēbant.
The slaves, because they were cowardly, were afraid of the ghost.
        Or:
Because the slaves were cowardly, they were afraid of the ghost.

3 Further examples:

1a Metella ad tablīnum festīnāvit.
1b Metella, postquam ē culīnā discessit, ad tablīnum festīnāvit.
2a amīcī Fēlīcem laudāvērunt.
2b amīcī, postquam fābulam audīvērunt, Fēlīcem laudāvērunt.
3a tuba sonuit.
3b postquam Rēgulus signum dedit, tuba sonuit.
4a Caecilius nōn erat sollicitus.
4b Caecilius nōn erat sollicitus, quod in cubiculō dormiēbat.
5a Nūcerīnī fūgērunt.
5b Nūcerīnī, quod Pompēiānī erant īrātī, fūgērunt.

PART TWO: Complete Vocabulary

1 Nouns and adjectives are usually listed in their nominative singular form, as follows:

servus   *slave*
magnus   *big, large, great*
ancilla   *slave-girl, slave-woman*
auxilium   *help*

2 3rd declension nouns, however, are listed with both nominative and accusative singular forms, as follows:

leō: leōnem   *lion*

This kind of entry means that **leō** is the nominative singular form and **leōnem** the accusative singular form of the Latin word for *lion*.
(Some of your friends in other schools may have textbooks that list a noun like **leō** as follows: **leō: leōnis**   *lion*. The form **leōnis** is genitive singular. You will learn this form in Stage 17. Notice that the accusative singular **leōnem** is different from the genitive singular **leōnis** in the final letters only.)

3 Practice examples

Find the nominative singular of the following words:

novāculam, lupum, sanguinem, parietem, cinerem
stēllae, īnfantēs, mūrō, cīvibus, mercātōrī.

4 Verbs are usually listed in the form of their present and perfect tenses, as follows:

parat   *prepares*: parāvit

This kind of entry indicates that **parat** means *s/he, it prepares* and **parāvit** means *s/he, it prepared* or *has prepared*.

5 If only one of these two tenses is used in Unit 1, then only that tense is listed.

For example: exspīrāvit   *died*

---

6 Practice examples

Find the meaning of the following words, some of which are in the present tense and some in the perfect:

laudat, laudāvit, respondit, respondet, intellēxit, accēpit

7 Some Latin words have more than one possible translation. Always choose the most suitable translation for the sentence you are working on.

cīvēs perterritī urbem petēbant.
The terrified citizens were heading for the city.

iuvenēs īrātī mercātōrem petīvērunt.
The angry young men attacked the merchant.

8 All words which are given in the "Words and Phrases Checklists" for Stages 1–12 are marked with an asterisk (*) in the following pages.

a

* abest   *is gone, is absent*
* abit   *goes away:* abiit
  accidit   *happened*
* accipit   *accepts:* accēpit
  accūsat   *accuses*
  āctor: āctōrem   *actor*
* ad   *to, at*
  addidit   *added*
* adest   *is here, is present*
  adiuvat   *helps*
  administrat   *manages*
  aedificat   *builds*
  aeger: aegrum   *sick, ill*
  Aegyptius   *Egyptian*
* agit   *does, acts*
*   fābulam agit   *acts in a play*
      grātiās agit   *thanks*
*   negōtium agit   *does business, works*
* agitat   *chases, hunts:* agitāvit
* agnōscit   *recognizes:* agnōvit
* agricola   *farmer*
  alius   *other, another*

alter: alterum   *the other, the second*
amat   *likes, loves*
* ambulat   *walks:* ambulāvit
* amīcus   *friend*
* āmittit   *loses:* āmīsit
  amphitheātrum   *amphitheater*
* ancilla   *slave-girl, slave-woman*
  animal   *animal*
  antīquus   *old, ancient*
* ānulus   *ring*
  anxius   *anxious*
  aper   *boar*
  aperit   *opens:* aperuit
  apodytērium   *changing-room*
  appāret   *appears:* appāruit
  architectus   *builder, architect*
  ardet   *burns, is on fire*
  arēna   *arena*
  argentāria   *banker's stall*
  argentārius   *banker*
  argūmentum   *proof, evidence*
  artifex: artificem   *artist, craftsman*

asinus   *ass, donkey*
āter: ātrum   *black*
āthlēta   *athlete*
* ātrium   *atrium, reception hall*
attonitus   *astonished*
auctor: auctōrem   *creator*
audācissimē   *very boldly*
* audit   *hears, listens to:* audīvit
aurae   *air*
auxilium   *help*
* avārus   *miser*

b

babae!   *hey!*
barba   *beard*
barbarus   *barbarian*
basilica   *court building*
benignus   *kind*
bēstia   *wild animal, beast*
bēstiārius   *a gladiator who fights animals, beast-fighter*
* bibit   *drinks:* bibit

c

caelum   *sky*
caldārium   *hot room*
* callidus   *clever, smart*
candidātus   *candidate*
* canis: canem   *dog*
cantat   *sings:* cantāvit
* capit   *takes:* cēpit
caudex: caudicem   *blockhead, idiot*
caupō: caupōnem   *innkeeper*
cautē   *cautiously*
cavea   *seating area*
cēlat   *hides:* cēlāvit
* celebrat   *celebrates*
* celeriter   *quickly*
   quam celerrimē   *as quickly as possible*
* cēna   *dinner*
* cēnat   *eats dinner, dines:* cēnāvit
* centuriō: centuriōnem   *centurion*
cēpit   *took, has taken*
* cēra   *wax, wax tablet*
cervus   *deer*
Chrīstiānus   *Christian*
* cibus   *food*
* cinis: cinerem   *ash*

* circumspectat   *looks around:* circumspectāvit
* cīvis: cīvem   *citizen*
* clāmat   *shouts:* clāmāvit
* clāmor: clāmōrem   *shout, uproar*
clausit   *shut, closed*
clausus   *closed*
cōgitat   *considers*
columba   *dove, pigeon*
commīsit   *began*
commōtus   *moved, affected*
* complet   *fills*
compōnit   *arranges*
comprehendit   *arrested*
cōnfēcit   *finished*
cōnsentit   *agrees*
cōnsilium   *plan, idea*
   cōnsilium capit   *makes a plan, has an idea*
* cōnspicit   *catches sight of:* cōnspexit
* cōnsūmit   *eats:* cōnsūmpsit
* contendit   *hurries:* contendit
contentiō: contentiōnem   *argument*
* contentus   *satisfied*
contrōversia   *debate*
* convenit   *gathers, meets*
convincit   *convicts, finds guilty*
* coquit   *cooks:* coxit
* coquus   *cook*
cotīdiē   *every day*
* crēdit   *trusts, believes, has faith in*
crīnēs: crīnēs   *hair*
* cubiculum   *bedroom*
cucurrit   *ran, has run*
culīna   *kitchen*
* cum   *with*
* cupit   *wants*
* cūr?   *why?*
cūrat   *takes care of*
   nihil cūrō   *I don't care*
* currit   *runs:* cucurrit
* custōdit   *guards*

d

* dat   *gives:* dedit
   fābulam dat   *puts on a play*
* dē   *down from; about*
dea   *goddess*
dēbet   *owes*
decem   *ten*

dēcidit *fell down*
dēcipit *deceives, tricks*
dedit *gave, has given*
dēiēcit *threw down*
deinde *then*
dēlectat *delights, pleases:* dēlectāvit
dēlēvit *destroyed*
dēliciae *darling*
dēnārius *a denarius (a small coin)*
* dēnsus *thick*
   dēnsior *thicker*
   dēnsissimus *very thick*
dēpōnit *puts down, takes off:* dēposuit
dēscendit *comes down*
dēsertus *deserted*
dēsistit *stops*
dēspērat *despairs*
dēstrīnxit *drew (a sword), pulled out*
deus *god*
dīcit *says:* dīxit
dictat *dictates*
* diēs: diem *day*
*   diēs nātālis: diem nātālem *birthday*
difficilis *difficult*
dīligenter *carefully*
discēdit *departs, leaves:* discessit
discit *learns*
discus *discus*
dissentit *disagrees, argues*
dīves: dīvitem *rich*
dīvīsor: dīvīsōrem *distributor, a man
   hired to bribe voters*
dīxit *said*
docet *teaches*
doctus *educated, skillful*
dolet *hurts, is in pain*
domina *lady (of the house), mistress*
* dominus *master (of the house)*
dōnum *present, gift*
* dormit *sleeps:* dormīvit
dubium *doubt*
* dūcit *leads:* dūxit
* duo *two*

e

* ē *out of, from*
eam *her*
ēbrius *drunk*
* ecce! *see! look!*
ēdit *presents:* ēdidit
effūgit *escaped*

* ego *I*
* ēheu! *alas! oh dear!*
ēlēgit *chose, has chosen*
* emit *buys:* ēmit
* ēmittit *throws, sends out:* ēmīsit
eōs *them*
* epistula *letter*
ērādit *erases:* ērāsit
erat *was*
* est *is*
ēsurit *is hungry*
* et *and*
* euge! *hurrah!*
* eum *him, it*
ēvānuit *vanished*
ēvītāvit *avoided*
ēvolāvit *flew*
ex *out of, from*
exanimātus *unconscious*
excitāvit *aroused, woke up*
* exclāmat *exclaims, shouts:* exclāmāvit
* exercet *exercises:* exercuit
* exit *goes out*
expedītus *lightly armed*
explicāvit *explained*
* exspectat *waits for*
exspīrāvit *died*
extrāxit *pulled out*

f

* fābula *play, story*
* facile *easily*
* facit *makes, does:* fēcit
familia *household*
fautor: fautōrem *supporter*
* favet *favors, supports*
fēcit *made, did*
fēlēs: fēlem *cat*
fēlīx: fēlīcem *lucky, happy*
* fēmina *woman*
* ferōciter *fiercely*
* ferōx: ferōcem *fierce, ferocious*
   ferōcissimus *very fierce*
* fert *brings, carries*
* festīnat *hurries:* festīnāvit
fidēlis *faithful, loyal*
filia *daughter*
* filius *son*
fīnis: fīnem *end*
* flamma *flame*
fluit *flows*

fortasse   *perhaps*
* fortis   *brave, strong*
    fortior   *braver, stronger*
    fortissimus   *very brave, very strong*
* fortiter   *bravely*
* forum   *forum, business center*
  frāctus   *broken*
* frāter: frātrem   *brother*
  fremit   *roars:* fremuit
* frūstrā   *in vain*
* fugit   *runs away, flees:* fūgit
  fūmus   *smoke*
  fūnambulus   *tightrope walker*
* fundus   *farm*
* fūr: fūrem   *thief*
  furcifer!   *scoundrel! crook!*
  fūstis: fūstem   *club, stick*

g

  garrit   *chatters, gossips*
* gēns: gentem   *family*
  gerit   *wears*
  gladiātor: gladiātōrem   *gladiator*
* gladius   *sword*
  Graecia   *Greece*
  Graeculus   *poor little Greek*
  Graecus   *Greek*
  grātiae   *thanks*
    grātiās agit   *gives thanks*
  graviter   *seriously*
* gustat   *tastes:* gustāvit

h

* habet   *has*
* habitat   *lives*
  hae   *these*
  haec   *this*
  hanc   *this*
  hausit   *drained, drank up*
* hercle!   *by Hercules!*
* heri   *yesterday*
  hī   *these*
* hic   *this*
  hoc   *this*
* hodiē   *today*
* homō: hominem   *person, man*
* hortus   *garden*
* hospes: hospitem   *guest*
  hūc   *here, to this place*
  hunc   *this*

i

* iacet   *lies, rests*
* iam   *now*
  iamprīdem   *a long time ago*
* iānua   *door*
  ībat   *was going*
  ibi   *there*
* igitur   *therefore, and so*
* ignāvus   *cowardly, lazy*
  illam   *that*
* ille   *that*
  imitātor: imitātōrem   *imitator*
* imperium   *empire*
  impetus   *attack*
  imprimit   *presses*
* in   *in, on; into, onto*
  incendium   *fire, blaze*
* incidit   *falls:* incidit
* incitat   *urges on, encourages*
  induit   *puts on*
* īnfāns: īnfantem   *baby, child*
  īnfēlīx: īnfēlīcem   *unlucky*
* ingēns: ingentem   *huge*
* inimīcus   *enemy*
* inquit   *says, said*
  īnsānus   *insane, crazy*
  īnscrīptiō: īnscrīptiōnem   *inscription, notice, writing*
* īnspicit   *looks at, inspects, examines:* īnspexit
  īnstitor: īnstitōrem   *peddler, street-vendor*
* intellegit   *understands:* intellēxit
* intentē   *intently*
  interfēcit   *killed*
* intrat   *enters:* intrāvit
  intrō īte!   *go inside!*
  intus   *inside*
* invenit   *finds:* invēnit
* invītat   *invites:* invītāvit
* īrātus   *angry*
  īrātior   *angrier*
    īrātissimus   *very angry*
  iste   *that*
* it   *goes:* iit
  ita   *in this way*
  ita vērō   *yes*
  iter   *journey, progress*
* iterum   *again*
  iubet   *orders*
* iūdex: iūdicem   *judge*
* iuvenis: iuvenem   *young man*

l

* labōrat   *works:* labōrāvit
* lacrimat   *cries, weeps*
  laetē   *happily*
* laetus   *happy*
    laetissimus   *very happy*
  lambit   *licks*
  lapideus   *made of stone*
  larārium   *domestic shrine*
  larēs   *household gods*
  latet   *lies hidden*
  Latīnus   *Latin*
  lātrat   *barks:* lātrāvit
* laudat   *praises:* laudāvit
  lectus   *couch*
* legit   *reads:* lēgit
* leō: leōnem   *lion*
* liber   *book*
* līberālis   *generous*
    līberālissimus   *very generous*
  līberāvit   *freed, set free*
  līberī   *children*
  lībertās: lībertātem   *freedom*
* lībertus   *freedman, ex-slave*
  lingua   *tongue, language*
  locus   *place*
  longē   *far, a long way*
  longus   *long*
    longissimus   *very long*
  lūcet   *shines*
  lūcidus   *bright*
  lūna   *moon*
  lupus   *wolf*

m

  magnificē   *splendidly, magnificently*
  magnificus   *splendid, magnificent*
* magnus   *big, large, great*
  maior   *bigger, larger, greater*
  māne   *in the morning*
* manet   *remains, stays:* mānsit
  marītus   *husband*
* māter: mātrem   *mother*
  maximus   *very big, very large, very great*
  mē   *me*
    mēcum   *with me*
* medius   *middle*
  melior   *better*
  mendācissimus   *very deceitful*
* mendāx: mendācem   *liar*
* mēnsa   *table*

* mercātor: mercātōrem   *merchant*
* meus   *my, mine*
  mihi   *to me*
* minimē!   *no!*
* mīrābilis   *marvelous, strange, wonderful*
  miserandus   *pitiful, pathetic*
  missiō: missiōnem   *release*
* mittit   *sends:* mīsit
* mōns: montem   *mountain*
  moribundus   *almost dead, dying*
  moritūrus   *going to die*
  mors: mortem   *death*
* mortuus   *dead*
* mox   *soon*
* multus   *much, (in pl.) many*
  murmillō: murmillōnem   *a kind of*
    gladiator
* mūrus   *wall*

n

* nārrat   *tells, relates:* nārrāvit
  nāsus   *nose*
  nauta   *sailor*
* nāvis: nāvem   *ship*
* necat   *kills:* necāvit
  negōtium   *business*
  nēmō: nēminem   *no one, nobody*
* nihil   *nothing*
    nihil cūrō   *I don't care*
  nimium   *too much*
  nisi   *except*
  nōbilis   *noble, of noble birth*
  nōbīs   *to us*
* nōn   *not*
* nōs   *we, us*
* noster: nostrum   *our*
* nōtus   *well known, famous*
    nōtissimus   *very well known, very*
    famous
  novācula   *(long) razor*
  novus   *new*
  nox: noctem   *night*
* nūbēs: nūbem   *cloud*
  Nūcerīnī   *people of Nuceria*
  nūllus   *no*
  nūm?   *surely . . . not?*
  numerat   *counts*
  numquam   *never*
* nunc   *now*
* nūntiat   *announces:* nūntiāvit
* nūntius   *messenger*

o

obdormīvit   *fell asleep*
obstinātē   *stubbornly*
occupātus   *busy*
* offert   *offers*
oleum   *oil*
olfēcit   *smelled, sniffed*
* ōlim   *once, some time ago*
* omnis   *all*
opportūnē   *just at the right time*
* optimē   *very well*
* optimus   *very good, excellent, best*
ōrātiō: ōrātiōnem   *speech*
ōre   *from its mouth*
* ostendit   *shows:* ostendit
ōtiōsus   *at leisure, with time off, idle*

p

* paene   *nearly, almost*
palaestra   *palaestra, exercise ground*
pānis: pānem   *bread*
* parat   *prepares:* parāvit
parātus   *ready*
parce!   *mercy!*
parēns: parentem   *parent*
pariēs: parietem   *wall*
* parvus   *small*
pāstor: pāstōrem   *shepherd*
* pater: patrem   *father*
* paulīsper   *for a short time*
pauper: pauperem   *poor*
    pauperrimus   *very poor*
pāvō: pāvōnem   *peacock*
pavor: pavōrem   *panic*
* pāx: pācem   *peace*
* pecūnia   *money*
* per   *through*
percussit   *struck*
perīculōsus   *dangerous*
perit   *dies, perishes:* periit
* perterritus   *terrified*
pervēnit   *reached, arrived at*
* pēs: pedem   *foot, paw*
pessimus   *worst, very bad*
* pestis: pestem   *pest, rascal*
* petit   *heads for, attacks, seeks:* petīvit
philosophus   *philosopher*
pictor: pictōrem   *painter, artist*
pictūra   *painting, picture*
pingit   *paints*
piscīna   *fishpond*

pistor: pistōrem   *baker*
* placet   *it pleases, suits*
* plaudit   *applauds, claps:* plausit
plēnus   *full*
plūrimus   *most*
* pōculum   *cup (often for wine)*
* poēta   *poet*
pollex: pollicem   *thumb*
Pompēiānus   *Pompeian*
pōns: pontem   *bridge*
* porta   *gate*
* portat   *carries:* portāvit
porticus   *colonnade*
* portus   *harbor*
* post   *after*
posteā   *afterwards*
* postquam   *after, when*
postrēmō   *finally, lastly*
postrīdiē   *(on) the next day*
* postulat   *demands:* postulāvit
posuit   *placed, put up*
praemium   *profit*
pretiōsus   *expensive, precious*
* prīmus   *first*
probat   *proves*
probus   *honest*
* prōcēdit   *advances, proceeds:* prōcessit
* prōmittit   *promises:* prōmīsit
* prope   *near*
proprius   *right, proper*
prōvocāvit   *called out, challenged*
proximus   *nearest*
* puella   *girl*
* puer   *boy*
pugil: pugilem   *boxer*
* pugna   *fight*
* pugnat   *fights:* pugnāvit
* pulcher: pulchrum   *beautiful*
    pulcherrimus   *very beautiful*
* pulsat   *hits, knocks on, whacks, punches:*
    pulsāvit
pȳramis: pȳramidem   *pyramid*

q

quadrāgintā   *forty*
* quaerit   *searches for, looks for:* quaesīvit
* quam   *than, how*
    quam celerrimē   *as quickly as possible*
quantī?   *how much?*
quid?   *what?*
quiētus   *quiet*
quīndecim   *fifteen*

quīnquāgintā *fifty*
quīnque *five*
* quis? *who?*
quō? *where, where to?*
* quod *because*
* quoque *also, too*

r

rādit *scrapes*
* rapit *seizes, grabs:* rapuit
recitat *recites*
* recumbit *lies down, reclines:* recubuit
recūsāvit *refused*
* reddit *gives back*
rediit *went back, came back, returned*
* rēs: rem *thing*
    rem cōgitat *considers the problem*
    rem cōnfēcit *finished the job*
    rem intellegit *understands the truth*
    rem nārrat *tells the story*
    rem probat *proves the case*
respīrāvit *recovered, revived*
* respondet *replies:* respondit
rētiārius *gladiator who fought with net*
retinet *holds back, keeps*
* revenit *comes back, returns*
rhētor: rhētorem *teacher*
* rīdet *laughs, smiles:* rīsit
rīdiculus *ridiculous, silly*
* rogat *asks:* rogāvit
Rōma *Rome*
Rōmānus *Roman*
ruīna *ruin, wreckage*
ruit *rushes:* ruit

s

sacrificium *offering, sacrifice*
* saepe *often*
salit *leaps, jumps*
salūs: salūtem *safety*
* salūtat *greets:* salūtāvit
* salvē! *hello!*
* sanguis: sanguinem *blood*
* satis *enough*
scaena *stage, scene*
scissus *torn*
scit *knows*
* scrībit *writes:* scrīpsit
scrīptor: scrīptōrem *sign-writer*
sculptor: sculptōrem *sculptor*

scurrīlis *obscene, dirty*
sē *himself, herself, themselves*
secat *cuts:* secuit
* secundus *second*
* sed *but*
* sedet *sits*
sella *chair*
sēmirutus *half-collapsed*
sēmisomnus *half-asleep*
* semper *always*
* senātor: senātōrem *senator*
* senex: senem *old man*
senior *older*
sēnsim *slowly, gradually*
* sententia *opinion*
* sentit *feels:* sēnsit
serpēns: serpentem *snake*
* servat *saves, protects:* servāvit
* servus *slave*
sibi *to himself*
* signum *sign, seal, signal*
* silva *woods, forest*
sine *without*
* sollicitus *worried, anxious*
* sōlus *alone, lonely*
sonuit *sounded*
sonus *sound*
sordidus *dirty*
soror: sorōrem *sister*
* spectāculum *show, spectacle*
* spectat *looks at, watches:* spectāvit
spectātor: spectātōrem *spectator*
spīna *thorn*
splendidus *splendid*
* stat *stands*
* statim *at once*
statua *statue*
stēlla *star*
stertit *snores*
stilus *pen, stick*
stola *(long) dress*
strigilis: strigilem *strigil, scraper*
* stultus *stupid*
stultior *more stupid*
stultissimus *very stupid*
suāviter *sweetly*
* subitō *suddenly*
* superat *overcomes, overpowers:*
    superāvit
superfuit *survived*
* surgit *gets up, rises:* surrēxit

---

suscipit *undertakes, takes on*
susurrāvit *whispered, mumbled*
* suus *his, her, their*
Syrius *Syrian*

t

* taberna *store, shop, inn*
tablīnum *study*
* tacet *is silent, is quiet:* tacuit
* tacitē *quietly, silently*
* tamen *however*
* tandem *at last*
tantum *only*
tē *you (singular)*
tēcum *with you (singular)*
* templum *temple*
tenet *holds*
tepidārium *warm room*
* terra *ground, land*
* terret *frightens:* terruit
* tertius *third*
testis: testem *witness*
theātrum *theater*
thermae *baths*
tibi *to you (singular)*
* timet *is afraid, fears:* timuit
timidē *fearfully*
titulus *advertisement, slogan*
toga *toga*
tondet *shaves, trims*
tōnsor: tōnsōrem *barber*
* tōtus *whole*
* trādit *hands over:* trādidit
trahit *drags:* trāxit
trānsfīxit *pierced*
tremor: tremōrem *trembling, tremor*
tremuit *trembled, shook*
* trēs *three*
triclīnium *dining-room*
trīgintā *thirty*
trīste *sadly*
trīstis *sad*
* tū *you (singular)*
* tuba *trumpet*
* tum *then*
tunica *tunic*
* turba *crowd*
turbulentus *rowdy, disorderly*
tūtus *safe*
* tuus *your, yours*

u

* ubi *where*
ubīque *everywhere*
ululāvit *howled*
* umbra *ghost, shadow*
* ūnus *one*
* urbs: urbem *city*
* ūtilis *useful*
ūtilissimus *very useful*
* uxor: uxōrem *wife*

v

vāgīvit *cried, wailed*
* valdē *very much, very*
* valē *good-by*
valedīxit *said good-by*
valet *feels well*
* vehementer *violently, loudly*
vēnābulum *hunting spear*
vēnālīcius *slave-dealer*
* vēnātiō: vēnātiōnem *hunt*
vēnātor: vēnātōrem *hunter*
* vēndit *sells*
* venit *comes:* vēnit
* verberat *strikes, beats:* verberāvit
versipellis: versipellem *werewolf*
versus *verse, line of poetry*
vertit *turned*
vexat *annoys*
* via *street*
vibrat *waves, brandishes*
victor: victōrem *victor, winner*
* videt *sees:* vīdit
vīgintī *twenty*
vīlicus *overseer, manager*
* vīlla *villa, (large) house*
* vīnum *wine*
* vir *man*
vīsitat *visits*
vīta *life*
* vituperat *finds fault with, tells off, curses:* vituperāvit
vīvit *is alive*
vōbīs *to you (plural)*
* vocat *calls:* vocāvit
* vōs *you (plural)*
vulnerāvit *wounded, injured*

Guide to Characters and Places

(The numeral in parentheses identifies the Stage in which the person or place is first featured.)

Actius (5): actor.

Aegyptius (adj.) (10): Egyptian.

Āfer (11): rich candidate for duovir, favored by Marcus Tullius and Grumio.

Alexander (10): Greek friend of Quintus.

Anthrāx (9): slave guarding clothes in the apodyterium of the baths.

Lūcius CAECILIUS Iūcundus (1): rich banker of Pompeii; husband of Metella and father of Quintus.

Celer (3): painter of mural.

Cerberus (1): dog belonging to Caecilius; named after the Greek mythological hellhound.

Clēmēns (1): slave of Caecilius.

Decēns (7): friend of Caecilius; killed perhaps by the ghost of the gladiator Pugnax.

Diodōrus (10): small brother of Alexander.

Fēlīx (6): freedman, or former slave, of Caecilius; saved Quintus when infant.

Gāius (7): friend of Quintus who liked hunting.

Graecia (4): Greece

Graecus (adj.) (4): Greek.

Grumiō (1): cook and slave in household of Caecilius.

Herculēs (3): Greek mythological hero shown in mural painted by Celer.

Hermogenēs (4): Greek merchant; borrowed money from Caecilius and did not pay it back.

Holcōnius (11): son of senator; candidate for duovir, favored by Quartus Tullius and Caecilius.

Īsis (12): Egyptian mother goddess worshiped by some Pompeians; was thought to have saved Julius from death.

Lūcius Caecilius IŪCUNDUS (1): cognomen of Caecilius, the banker.

Iūlius (12): Julius, friend of Caecilius; lived near Nuceria.

Lūcius (11): candidate for duovir; favored by farmers.

Lucriō (5): old man; master of Poppaea.

Marcellus (9): merchant; sold toga to Metella.

MARCUS Tullius (11): brother of Quartus Tullius.

Melissa (3): beautiful slave-girl; bought from Syphax by Caecilius.

Metella (1): wife of Caecilius; mother of Quintus.

Milō (9): famous athlete; his statue was set up in the palaestra.

Neptūnus (10): Neptune; Roman god of the sea.

Nūceria (8): town neighboring Pompeii.

Nūcerīnī (8): Nucerians, or people of Nuceria.

Pantagathus (3): barber.

Pompēiānus (adj.) (4): Pompeian, or resident of Pompeii.

Lūcius Spurius POMPŌNIĀNUS (11): cognomen of the alias assumed by the slave Grumio so that he could vote in the election.

Poppaea (5): slave-girl of Lucrio; girlfriend first of Grumio, later of Clemens.

Priscus (5): wealthy citizen who paid for producing a play.

Pugnāx (7): gladiator killed by lion.

QUĀRTUS Tullius (11): brother of Marcus Tullius.

Quīntus (1): son of Caecilius and Metella.

Rēgulus (8): Roman senator; lived near Nuceria.

Rōmānus (adj.) (8): Roman.

Sceledrus (9): fellow slave of Anthrax at the baths.

Sorex (5): actor.

Lūcius SPURIUS Pompōniānus (11): nomen of the alias assumed by Grumio.

Sulla (11): painter of wall slogans.

Syphāx (3): slave-dealer from Syria.

Syrius (adj.) (3): Syrian.

Theodōrus (10): Greek rhetoric teacher of Quintus and Alexander.

Thrasymachus (10): small brother of Alexander.

Marcus et Quārtus TULLIUS (11): nomen of two brothers; paid Sulla to paint political slogans.

Vesuvius (7): volcano near Pompeii; erupted in A.D.79.

Index of Cultural Topics

The page references are all to the background sections at the ends of the Stages. You will also find cultural information in the Latin stories.

Index of Grammatical Topics

Key: AL = About the Language   RvG = Review Grammar

Page references are given first, with paragraph references (i.e. references to numbered sections in the language notes and the Review Grammar) following in boldface.

In general, AL references are only to the *first* language note on the grammatical topic in question; in a few cases, additional pages are cited.

Time Chart

B.C.	POMPEII	ROME	THE WORLD	B.C.
c. 3100–1166			Egypt ruled by Pharaohs	c. 3100–1166
c. 2100			Indo-European migrations	c. 2100
c. 1500			Minoan civilization at its height	c. 1500
c. 1450			Development of Hinduism	c. 1450
c. 1200			Exodus of Jews from Egypt	c. 1200
753		Foundation of Rome (traditional date) and rule of kings		753
700–600	Greek merchants settle in Pompeii			700–600
c. 563			Buddha born in India	c. 563
c. 551			Confucius born in China	c. 551
c. 530	Etruscans control Pompeii			c. 530
509		Expulsion of kings and founding of Roman Republic		509
500–400			{ Persian invasions of Greece / Golden Age of Athens	500–400
474	Samnites capture Pompeii			474
390		Rome briefly captured by Gauls		390
336			Alexander becomes ruler of Greece	336
300–200	Roman armies defeat Samnites	{ Rome gains control of Italy / Wars with Carthage	Building of Great Wall of China	300–200
218		Hannibal crosses the Alps		218
200–100		Rome extends rule outside Italy		200–100
90–80	Pompeii rebels against Romans			90–80
80	Pompeii becomes Roman colony			80
58–49		Caesar conquers Gaul		58–49
49		Caesar made "Dictator"		49
44		Caesar is murdered		44
44–31		Civil War between Octavian (Augustus) and Antony		44–31
27		Augustus becomes Emperor		27
c. 4		Birth of Jesus		c. 4

A.D.	POMPEII	ROME	THE WORLD	A.D.
14		Tiberius becomes Emperor		14
c. 29			Crucifixion of Jesus	*c.* 29
37		Caligula becomes Emperor		37
41		Claudius becomes Emperor		41
42		St Peter brings Christianity to Rome		42
45–57			Missionary journeys of St Paul	45–57
54		Nero becomes Emperor		54
59	Pompeians and Nucerians riot (*Stage 8*)			59
62	Earthquake damages parts of Pompeii			62
64		Great Fire at Rome; persecution of Christians by Nero		64
69		{ Year of Four Emperors / Vespasian becomes Emperor }		69
70			Sack of Jerusalem and Temple	70
79	{ March: Elections in Pompeii (*Stage 11*) / August 24: Vesuvius erupts (*Stage 12*) }	Titus becomes Emperor		79
81		Domitian becomes Emperor		81
96		Nerva becomes Emperor		96
98		Trajan becomes Emperor		98
117		Hadrian becomes Emperor		117
313			Emperor Constantine officially supports Christianity in Roman Empire	313
330			Capital of Roman Empire moved to Constantinople	330
410		Visigoths sack Rome		410
476		Last Emperor of Rome deposed		476

A.D.	POMPEII	ROME	THE WORLD	A.D.
570			Birth of Mohammed	570
800			Charlemagne crowned Emperor of Holy Roman Empire	800
800–1100		Period of turmoil in Italy		800–1100
1143		Rome becomes an independent city-state		1143
c. 1400		The Renaissance begins in Italy		c. 1400
1453			Turks capture Constantinople	1453
1492			Columbus arrives in America	1492
1497			Cabot explores Canada	1497
1521			Reformation begins	1521
1594	Fontana rediscovers Pompeii			1594
1620			Pilgrims land at Plymouth, Massachusetts	1620
1748	Charles III King of Naples conducts treasure-hunts in Pompeii			1748
1776			United States declare their Independence	1776
1806			End of Holy Roman Empire	1806
1815			Napoleon finally defeated at Waterloo	1815
1860	Fiorelli begins systematic excavations of Pompeii			1860
1861		Victor Emmanuel II becomes King of a united Italy		1861
1863			Lincoln emancipates American slaves	1863
1867			Canada becomes a Dominion	1867
1914–1918			First World War	1914–1918
1931			Canada becomes a Commonwealth nation	1931
1939–1945			Second World War	1939–1945
1944	Most recent eruption of Vesuvius			1944
1946		Italy becomes a Republic		1946

Reference Grammar

I   Forms (including some forms introduced later in the course)

I.1   NOUNS

	first declension	*second declension*	*third declension*	
SINGULAR				
nominative	**puella**	**servus**	**mercātor**	**leō**
genitive	**puellae**	**servī**	**mercātōris**	**leōnis**
dative	**puellae**	**servō**	**mercātōrī**	**leōnī**
accusative	**puellam**	**servum**	**mercātōrem**	**leōnem**
ablative	**puellā**	**servō**	**mercātōre**	**leōne**
PLURAL				
nominative	**puellae**	**servī**	**mercātōrēs**	**leōnēs**
genitive	**puellārum**	**servōrum**	**mercātōrum**	**leōnum**
dative	**puellīs**	**servīs**	**mercātōribus**	**leōnibus**
accusative	**puellās**	**servōs**	**mercātōrēs**	**leōnēs**
ablative	**puellīs**	**servīs**	**mercātōribus**	**leōnibus**

I.2   VERBS

	first conjugation	*second conjugation*	*third conjugation*	*third conjugation "-iō"*	*fourth conjugation*
PRESENT TENSE					
I carry	**portō**	**doceō**	**trahō**	**capiō**	**audiō**
you (sg.) carry	**portās**	**docēs**	**trahis**	**capis**	**audīs**
s/he, it carries	**portat**	**docet**	**trahit**	**capit**	**audit**
we carry	**portāmus**	**docēmus**	**trahimus**	**capimus**	**audīmus**
you (pl.) carry	**portātis**	**docētis**	**trahitis**	**capitis**	**audītis**
they carry	**portant**	**docent**	**trahunt**	**capiunt**	**audiunt**
IMPERFECT TENSE					
I was carrying	**portābam**	**docēbam**	**trahēbam**	**capiēbam**	**audiēbam**
you (sg.) were carrying	**portābās**	**docēbās**	**trahēbās**	**capiēbās**	**audiēbās**
s/he, it was carrying	**portābat**	**docēbat**	**trahēbat**	**capiēbat**	**audiēbat**
we were carrying	**portābāmus**	**docēbāmus**	**trahēbāmus**	**capiēbāmus**	**audiēbāmus**
you (pl.) were carrying	**portābātis**	**docēbātis**	**trahēbātis**	**capiēbātis**	**audiēbātis**
they were carrying	**portābant**	**docēbant**	**trahēbant**	**capiēbant**	**audiēbant**
PERFECT TENSE					
I carried	**portāvī**	**docuī**	**trāxī**	**cēpī**	**audīvī**
you (sg.) carried	**portāvistī**	**docuistī**	**trāxistī**	**cēpistī**	**audīvistī**
s/he, it carried	**portāvit**	**docuit**	**trāxit**	**cēpit**	**audīvit**
we carried	**portāvimus**	**docuimus**	**trāximus**	**cēpimus**	**audīvimus**
you (pl.) carried	**portāvistis**	**docuistis**	**trāxistis**	**cēpistis**	**audīvistis**
they carried	**portāvērunt**	**docuērunt**	**trāxērunt**	**cēpērunt**	**audīvērunt**

II   Subordinate Clauses

In Unit I, you have met several examples of subordinate clauses. A subordinate clause is one that cannot stand by itself, but is dependent on (i.e. subordinate to) the rest of the sentence, which is called the main clause. You have seen subordinate clauses introduced by the words **quod**, meaning *because*, **postquam**, meaning *after*, and **ubi**, meaning *where*. Study the following examples, in which the subordinate clauses are in boldface.

II.1   Grumiō cibum cōnsūmpsit, **quod dominus dormiēbat.**
Grumio ate the food, ***because his master was sleeping.***

fūr, **quod perterritus erat,** ē vīllā fūgit.
The thief fled from the villa, ***because he was terrified.***

II.2   **postquam servī portās aperuērunt,** leōnēs arēnam intrāvērunt.
The lions entered the arena ***after the slaves opened the gates.***

fēminae, **postquam stolās ēmērunt,** ē tabernā discessērunt.
After they bought the dresses, *the women left the store.*

II.3   Melissa triclīnium intrāvit, **ubi Quīntus et amīcī cēnābant.**
Melissa entered the dining-room, ***where Quintus and his friends were eating dinner.***

III   Sentence Patterns

Below are some of the most important sentence patterns which you have met in Unit I. The patterns are shown on the left, with examples given on the right.
Key: NOM = nominative; ACC = accusative; DAT = dative; V = verb.

PATTERNS	EXAMPLES
III.1 NOM + est + predicate (noun or adjective)	Melissa est ancilla *Melissa is a slave-girl.*
III.2 NOM + ACC +V	dominus coquum laudāvit. *The master praised the cook.*
III.3 interrogative word (quis, quid, cūr, ubi) + NOM + V	quid tū cupis? *What do you want?*
III.4 NOM + subordinate clause (see section II) + ACC + V	cīvēs, quod tremōrēs sentiēbant, auxilium quaerēbant. *The citizens looked for help, because they felt the tremors.*
III.5 NOM + DAT +ACC +V	Syphāx caupōnī ānulum dedit. *Syphax gave the ring to the innkeeper.*
III.6 NOM + DAT + V	mercātōrēs Holcōniō favent. *The merchants support Holconius.*
III.7 NOM + subordinate clause (expanded to contain DAT + ACC + V) + ACC + V	fēminae, postquam mercātōrī pecūniam dedērunt, togam cēpērunt. *The women took the toga, after they gave money to the merchant.*